To my family
who waited patiently
for me to just finish 'this one last idea'
every day

for months.

Specific ©2019 Adam Pierno   *978-0-9993990-1-9*

SPECIFIC

Adam Pierno

How brands draw
inspiration from a
world that doesn't
want any more

978-0-9993990-1-9

978-0-9993990-1-9

What is a "specific brand?"
It is a company that knows
who its best customer is
and builds everything it
says and does around
that customer. This may
alienate some people who
have a different point of
view. That is the exact
point. The specific brand
exists to please its
customer, and grows when
it can inspire more people
to become customers
based on that happy group
of core customers.

Introduction

Specific : Adam Pierno

INTRO-DUCTION

Once upon a time, there was a clear path to success for brands. It involved print spreads in international magazines, celebrity endorsements, and of course, television ads during the most watched shows and events of the year. This was still true only ten years ago. Now you can count the number of brands able to afford this type of program while reaching its best prospects on two hands and maybe one foot.

The number of advertisers willing and able to keep up with this level of campaign relates to changes to how people are taking it all in. Once, we all watched the same thing, and as a by-product we all saw the same ads. But that has all changed. The ratings for the most watched show on the air—Super Bowl broadcasts—have been dropping steadily for the past three years. The Oscars (traditionally the second most watched event each year) have been down for that same period and struggling since the late 1990s. There are fewer and fewer places and events that attract all of a population or even a meaningful minority.

Spend some time browsing a list of the most popular programming and you'll notice that there is a lot of content that applies to someone who is not you. The chief reason brands aren't able to predictably grow as large as they once did is there are fewer ways to reach audiences of that same scale. This is the great contradiction of modern marketing. Brands need to be specific with their messaging and targeting to be relevant. But brands must reach a broad audience if they want to grow. The most accessible and hyped media are digital platforms that sell discrete, tight targeting of existing customers or the category aware. Buying a broad audience is criticized as wasteful. In traditional media terms, over spray is not necessarily waste. An ad for a healthy meal service appearing in US Weekly will reach some people who have been shopping the category; as well as those unaware of the product and just looking at celebrity bikini photos; who suddenly find themselves more receptive to diet and health messaging.

There are infinite media options. There have never been more ways for brands to express themselves. Yet it has never been easier for a brand to blend in. Have you ever noticed that each new platform has a visual sensibility that most brands conform to? When you read the word 'Pinterest' you get a mental picture of what the content will look like. This applies to Instagram and Snapchat as well. You can picture a clear difference in the type of content you see on each and how it differs. If you thought about Reddit, you might imagine clumsily designed memes.

For the life of me, I cannot explain why brands deliberately melt into these platform conventions. They see something that works and they drift a little closer to that with every post, every new content calendar. If you scroll your entire Instagram timeline, you start to get the feeling there are only a handful of individuals creating every single post on the platform.

Have you ever seen *The Breakfast Club*? It is the story of a brain, an athlete, a basket case, a princess and a criminal. Do you know how John Hughes chose those groups? Because in 1985 that's all the options people had. Today, we have access to so many more things to be interested in, and so many ways to remix subjects, genres, styles and technology. The amount of descriptions can be broken up into so many more when they make the inevitable *Breakfast Club* reboot. In the 2025 version, they could have an entire room of types, mixing and matching the plethora of modern predominate character attributes.

For 10 years, there wasn't a single brand presentation without the words 'sea of sameness' on at least one slide. Now, brands and agencies fight over the oars to row out into those same waters. On the off chance you see something different in your social media feed, you remember it, don't you? You take note. Because it stands apart.

This logic has worked for television advertising for decades. Old Spice's Man Your Man Could Smell Like rejuvenated the brand because it was unlike anything airing at that time. What did 20 other consumer packaged goods brands do after its success? They created imitation ads featuring a spokesperson walking left to right across the screen making jokes about the category conventions. But not actually disrupting them, entirely missing Jean-Marie Dru's point. In his classic book *Disruption*, Mr. Dru defines the way to identify the conventions in a category—everything the competitive set does in the same way—to uncover opportunities to stand out.

When someone says television ad or billboard there is no mental image of what those things look like in their finished form. Add the name of a brand featured in the advertisement and the picture reveals itself. Funny, our understanding of the brand usually drives the way our mind imagines the ad, and not the media format. And remember shopping malls? Until the mid-90s, all stores were extremely limited in their outward experience. Retailers were allotted a space for signage and a choice of door openings that matched the appearance of the mall surroundings. Think about Abercrombie & Fitch or Hollister's beach porch storefront, playing music. Now fairly commonplace, it was revolutionary for brands to stand out via experiential entryways in the late 1990s.

A successful company has to find the way to make people take note of it. How to make people remember it. How to make people mentally bookmark your brand instead of a competitor. Better yet, to convince people to believe that there is no direct competitor, because no one can do what your company does for them in the exact way you do it. The way companies grow has changed dramatically. This is a result of changes in production and distribution. It is also due to the complex behavioral changes around media consumption and the explosion of options for consumers. Instead of bludgeoning people with mass reach advertising, a company could micro-target its core group of targets if it so chooses.

But a brand can only grow so big if it serves the same small constituency. There have also been countless examples of brands that failed by trying to widen appeal beyond a strong central group of people who believe in the brand and never quite outgrow that first audience. These are crazy times. Yet where do brands continue to look for inspiration on growth and audience capture? Other brands.

Every day, more dimensions get carved into the shape of media. There are more corners for brands to build a protected foundation. Instead, most brands work tirelessly to smooth out the edges and disappear into the standard. Whatever that standard might be. They strive to look like other brands they deem successful.

A *company* is defined in generic terms. Mercedes-Benz is a car company. Starbucks, a coffee company. But a *brand* is differentiated by definition. This book is about what needs to be defined. What needs to be specific about your company and how you serve your customers that makes it a brand. Brands fail when they lose their focus. Many brands become trained on what the rest of the category is doing. Or what global brands that have already achieved growth are doing. Instead, focus on the best customer and focus on how to excite them.

Truth time. Your product means nothing to people nor should it. It is just a hunk of plastic or bits of food that serve a utility purpose. To nourish, to shave, to fix, to entertain. Consumers use the product, eat the food or engage as directed, then walk away until they need to think about fulfilling that need again. If a product isn't emotional, then why do people love brands? That is the job of the external pieces that make up your brand. Your logo. Your people. Your advertising. The brand needs to be designed to appeal to a core group of specific people who will be most receptive to it and not alienate the next group of people they might tell about it.

The size and shape of brand has changed and will continue to change. There are fewer giant brands built every year, but there is more opportunity to create companies with brand differentiation than the year before. Even when mass reach was more likely, brands had to fight the temptation to be all things to all people, and often failed. A new company may be tempted to look to brands that have already achieved mass reach as a model. This is flawed because that scale may no longer be attainable in many categories, and the path most of those global brands took to the top have been wiped clean. Instead, today's companies need to seek inspiration elsewhere. True, there are some brands that can sell to just about everyone. A growing brand just needs to be understood by a core group before it can sell to another, or it risks confusing both groups.

In the 90's, McDonald's probably had a brand wheel, pillars, pyramid and fifty other Power Point doodads that existed in its headquarters about all the ways that McDonald's was a unique and beautiful snowflake. They invested millions in research and converted it into detailed communications sub-messages that outlined how no one else could deliver what McDonald's delivered. They were framed behind lucite and hung in break rooms in every restaurant. And yet, they were spending billions on mass television and print, so they had to find the attributes that were most attractive to the largest possible audience watching network television and MTV.

All the nuance never made it to the screen. Which means it never made it to consumers. Instead of the details of a great McDonald's experience, we got a singing Ronald McDonald and Jason Alexander dancing with his McDLT. Cut to the next generation of restaurants and how fast casual restaurants have entered the market and become dominant (for a time).

Chipotle's growth came from a steady diet of details. They not only wanted to tell customers the beans they use are organic, they provided the name of the farm. And the farmer. Details matter in differentiation. It is at least part of the reason why Chipotle outperformed rivals like Qdoba. Qdoba provided a very similar product but few of the memorable details that created dedicated cult appeal. Customers have no idea where Qdoba sourced their beans. Most people don't care, but for people that do, the information is huge. The mere idea that a company, especially one the size of Chipotle, would care enough to disclose is important.

Niman Ranch is one of the providers of Chipotle's pork. Awareness of Niman Ranch is probably 1% of Chipotle's among US consumers. Chipotle didn't promote their partnership to gain new customers already loyal to Niman Ranch's pork products. They slipped customers that detail to help them understand a pillar of their brand: responsible food sourcing. They use their bags to tell the story of discovering Niman Ranch, the partnership, the ethics. Chipotle uses long copy to share these details, and only when they know customers might read them. While they're eating.

But why were these details so important to Chipotle's growth when McDonald's grew with so few? The closest McDonald's got to this level of detail is the USDA seal in reference to their beef. Any ads about sourcing were more flag-waving propaganda than detailed disclosures. Reassurance more than education.

Times were different. Channels were different. Shopping was different. People thought about things differently.

Every brand starts as a company that reaches a particular customer. It only becomes a brand when the company earns a meaning beyond the product or service it sells. Meaning is communicated through details. Details are easy for someone to tell their friends about. Getting the right details to the right people is what successful brands do.

Why are locksmiths almost never brands? Because they have always sold a core service and nothing more. They have remained locked in a transactional Yellow Pages battle for the next paying customer since the dawn of time and through the digital era. Few have chosen to invest in a brand based on things consumers value beyond — "Oh shit, I'm locked out. Come help me."

But they are specific aren't they? Google 'locksmith' and you'll see they show hours, proximity, products and rates. Very detailed. But not specific where it matters. What higher order benefit do they serve? And if they identify one, what is the benefit they alone serve in the category?

Locksmiths are a commodity. Who made it so? Consumers who pushed prices down by taking advantage of ample competition or providers who never rose above the competitive din with a meaningful brand proposition?

Both are responsible in part. What is true for locksmiths is also true for most professional services companies. They chase capabilities with little regard for brand. Those capabilities become commodities because there is no differentiation. What does any locksmith do that no other one does — or that's worth telling someone about? Price becomes the primary lever, especially now that technology has rendered location less and less important. What is unique about your accountant? What makes them selectable?

Consumers have their role to play as well. Though a company attempts to communicate through a brand to differentiate itself and avoid commoditization, the consumer processes those signals through experience. We have many more feelings about the McDonald's brand or the Uber brand than any locksmith. Because we've had many more experiences with those brands, good and bad.

Consumers get to decide whether the brand signals are true or false. And to what degree. If an Uber rider has several trips in a week's time that she rates 5-stars, her impression of the brand likely rises. The next time she needs to summon a ride she's more likely to choose Uber than a competitor. Experience leads to belief in or rejection of the brand.

Services like locksmiths lack the frequency to build those experiences. A consumer calls a locksmith only when needed. Someone comes to the house, knocks out the work, provides a bill and leaves. If the job is done correctly, there won't be another experience for a long time.

It is more likely for a locksmith to damage their brand during a visit than to improve it. The nature of reviews dictates it. Beyond the very few super-users of review sites, angry people and elated people post the most reviews. How often do you think customers are elated by a commoditized service like replacing a lock? But, if the locksmith is late, or is missing a part, or miscommunicated the price when quoting, there is now an angry customer to reckon with. As the meme goes: You had one job.

If a customer can reduce you down to one job, and not to a higher order benefit, your company had better execute that single job flawlessly. Realistically, no customer will search for 'peace of mind' in Google. And next to nobody will search for a locksmith brand by name. They will search for the category: locksmith. That is a byproduct of media fragmentation and commoditization, the way they have worked together to make branding more challenging than ever.

In the early days of Google, a locksmith could create a website that would follow the documented and undocumented rules of SEO and make its way into search results. A search of the category would help customers find a business. No more. Search for 'pizza' and Google serves a list of global, national, and regional brands (in that order). Pizza Hut, Domino's, Papa John's, Papa Murphy's, Chuck E. Cheese's, Marco's, Famous Famiglia, Jet's, Spinato's, Peter Piper Pizza. Somewhere later are frozen brands like DiGiorno, Red Baron and Tombstone. Sprinkled in are also pages of other search and ratings results. There are multiple Yelp results for nearby ZIP codes. For a new pizza restaurant to be found—and to stand out—amongst these results takes nearly a miracle. Even searching 'pizza near me' produces a map cluttered with name brands that answer the customer need before they need to consider a new option. This is a problem for businesses since search is a dominant mechanism for consumer discovery and most marketing starts here.

It is also an opportunity. As ever, when an entire industry is pointing in the same direction there must be a road less traveled. Fighting for a spot on a list of companies using the word 'pizza' or 'locksmith' is futile.

People have been given tools to search for products in a number a ways, not just by brand name. They can search for the problem they are having and choose a product. They can choose from a filtered set of only 5-star reviews. They can buy a product without ever seeing it or identifying a brand through an Echo device. But companies trying to become brands today are still using the same reference points from the same case studies. They are still following the same playbook used by Mr. Clean and Tropicana. As people have learned to find solutions without leading with a brand name, they have begun to rely on brand names less.

Companies willing to get specific will differentiate and flourish. For a company to become a special brand, trusted by its customers and finding new ones, they need to use new models for how people search and find things they love today.

Specific : Adam Pierno

LET'S GET SPECIFIC

What is specific? Just using more descriptive words? No. Being more clear? Not exactly. To understand what is meant by specific, let's explore another word: niche. A niche brand is designed to meet the needs of only a portion of a market. A product may have a key feature to appeal to core users of a category, or a service may be tailored to meet the needs of a subset of the category audience. Here are two niche brands aimed at men.

Stubble & Stache is a moisturizer brand for men — less than half the market for moisturizer. But not all men; these products are positioned for men with facial hair. And not just men *with* facial hair; men committed to it. Everything about the product line claims to soothe skin and soften and condition facial hair and stubble. Pushing it further into niche territory, the product was developed by a US Marine as a tribute to a fallen comrade. It appeals most to US veterans with facial hair.

Mtailor is a service that uses technology to allow men to capture their measurements for better fitting clothing. The niche here is not just men, but men inclined to custom clothing or who have had difficulty buying clothes that fit properly off the rack at major retailers. It also requires faith in the technology, which is less of a barrier now than it was when the service launched. Cleverly, Mtailor is expanding beyond its niche with an initial product for women; jeans. A smart niche play because jeans are notoriously hard to shop for and choose due to oddities in brand sizing and fit.

Meanwhile, smaller brands use the word (often incorrectly) to explain their smaller revenue numbers, penetration or growth. As many have pointed out, a niche is a limit to growth. The niche is narrow and does not have a built-in mass audience. It has the opposite definition: a small audience that is highly interested. Underachieving brands use 'niche' as a crutch, while the reality is that an intelligently deployed niche is an advantage for building a company that can grow roots.

The definition of 'niche brand' hasn't changed, but it seems larger brands now use the word *niche* to demean and marginalize smaller rivals. It is used by global brands to say "this competitor is not big enough to be a threat, or lacks the mass appeal necessary to unseat category leaders like us." They diminish the brand by saying they only speak to a small group out of the total market. In other words, they will tell us that niche is something they wish to avoid being. But that is not the behavior they demonstrate.

Coca-Cola is a product known by almost every human being on earth since the 1950s. That is a testament to their branding and advertising prowess. The most amazing part? The Coca-Cola company is built around a nearly 120-year-old product that has never had a true benefit. It is sweetened water.

The Coca-Cola Company's flagship brand uses its red can for awareness but also offers dozens of individual products based on flavor, carbonation, mouthfeel, packaging and local preference. Each of those carry a smaller niche audience that many other brands would kill for. In some cases, they create niche products aimed at demographic groups. In the 90's they launched OK Soda, a soft drink brand aimed at the then young Generation X. The cans featured curiosity-inducing artwork by illustrator Daniel Clowes and the ad campaign was a series of non-ads aimed at cynical twentysomethings. I collected the cans despite hating the beverage, so in a sense, the product got through to me. I remember it 25 years later.

Amazon is a huge company that provides access to millions of niche brands and products. It grows by creating dozens of small niches that it attempts to grow into mass products and services. They build products with an initial niche audience and learn how to expand it to other people. In a lot of cases, the first niche group is Amazon employees. They build their own solutions to solve a problem they know exists inside Amazon, and later figure out if other companies or individuals would want this too. This is how we ended up with Key and many of Amazon's other smaller businesses.

Not everyone drinks Coca-Cola classic. Not everyone uses every Amazon service. But everyone drinks something and Coca-Cola probably makes a few products that everyone can choose. OK Soda was a niche play that failed. It failed because it acted like a mass brand.

Huge global companies have a choice. They can make their brand stand for meeting the thirst needs of people wherever they are or some generic "mission" like that, or they can dial in closer and closer to a smaller group of people with a better defined need: A sweet carbonated cola drink made for sharing. A cola flavored drink for the calorie concerned. A cola flavored drink for those seeking to avoid calories and sugar. A diet cola flavored drink for those avoiding artificial sweeteners.

Notice what happens to product descriptions as Coca-Cola moves toward niches. *They get more and more specific*. You couldn't sell meeting generic thirst needs to everyone in every convenience store, although they made a great run at it for 50 years. Notice something else: not only does the product description get tighter; but with each sub-product, the description of the customer gets more defined. This is how products become brands. An extremely well-defined product or feature for a well defined audience. Being specific is not thinking small, being specific is making tight connections.

Gillette has been a powerhouse in shaving products for decades. Mass producing blades behind highly protected patents that protect proprietary blade manufacturing 'technology.' They showered consumers with deeply focus grouped creative and a blade count arms race that became a parody of itself. Five blades in a disposable razor? Really? Stop reading and think about any Gillette ad you can remember.

Here is what you pictured: a man standing at a sink. Good looking. Wearing a towel. Swipes the razor down his entire right cheek. Cut to a CGI rendering of the components of a razor coming together, metal glinting. The man touches his smooth face. Alt: A woman touches his smooth face. Pretty close to what you pictured?

That sums up four decades of Gillette ads. Until 2017. That year, Gillette started communicating about heritage, about staff, about Massachusetts. Gillette started using real employees to tell the story of American manufacturing and commitment to excellence. They provide the name and location of the employee. They use a version of the employees own words. In ad copy, they talk about Gillette's relationship to the local economy. They are adding specifics. And now, they've launched a new interpretation of "The Best a Man Can Get" via television and video that focuses on toxic masculinity. The campaign is designed to tap into emotion, to make the brand more than a producer of plastic razors and something worth having a conversation about.

Why? Because they are losing share at a terrifying rate. Dollar Shave Club launched and used a few well-placed details to poke holes in Gillette's business. Details like the actual margin of producing and selling blades and blade refills on a quasi-subscription basis. Dollar Shave Club pointed out to consumers how much more they were paying than they needed to.

Dollar Shave Club wasn't the only brand to chip away at Gillette's myth. Harry's also launched with some details that hurt Gillette. They began sharing details about the lengths Gillette (along with Schick) went to in order to keep other companies for mass-producing blades for shaving. Guess what else they were sharing details on? The factory, the sourcing of the steel, the heritage. Sound familiar? They communicated details that gave people looking for a reason to choose a razor brand—rather than merely adopt a company—the information they needed. A German factory, speaking to precision. Swedish steel, referencing the high purity iron ore Swedes have been working with since the 13th century. These aren't just copy details. They are details that drive brand difference and a reason to choose them.

While Harry's tone and style is factual and engineering-focused, Dollar Shave Club is glib and fun. They provide details to parody the way big shaving brands have been fleecing consumers for decades. The details each brand chooses to share align with, and in some cases drive the tone of the brand. The alignment between the facts and the tone is what makes them specific.

For a time, Gillette referred to both Dollar Shave Club and Harry's as niche brands. And they meant it to be dismissive. The products of all three companies are remarkably similar. Metal blades in plastic handles. Soap. Moisturizer. In what way would those products be described as niche? How could they when they're essentially identical to the mass brand, Gillette? These niche brands don't create niche products. But like most of the beverages in the Coca-Cola portfolio, they do appeal to niche audience.

Every great niche brand has a monopoly on its offering. They are not the only company selling the product or service. They are the only company offering the specific combination of product, benefit and promise. They perform in a way that makes them unique or special. Any drink company could make a grapefruit flavored soda, but only Coca-Cola makes Fresca. As seen above, the products of our three shaving brands are so similar that Gillette sued to keep those of the smaller brands out of the US. But the brands served niche audiences.

Dollar Shave Club launched to serve very practical guys. These are men who think "I have to shave no matter what, it's a life tax. I may as well make that tax as low as possible." *That tax* can apply to the cost of razors (Gillette is more expensive) or the initial benefit of regularly timed delivery which offered convenience (Gillette ignored this mail order business for years). Cheaper and more convenient. That does not sound like a small niche audience does it? Dollar Shave Club saw the potential past the smaller subset of early adopters.

Harry's launched to serve men looking to get back to basics. These are men who think "I want products that are designed to work for me, I don't want expensive, one-size-fits-all products." Harry's bought a German factory to become their own supplier, simplify product design and manufacturing and drive cost down. Their customers appreciate the bespoke nature of the razors in comparison to Gillette's mass-produced ilk.

Many companies around the world produce razors. None have a monopoly or operate without competition, especially now. But brands operating specifically have a monopoly on what their exact consumer wants, needs and is happy to buy. As they expand to reach more audience, they often lose what made them special to that initial customer group.

If you are at all familiar with Dollar Shave Club, you're shaking your fist at this book as you read. "But that brand was acquired by Unilever for a billion dollars! That hardly qualifies as a niche brand you [expletive]!" It's true. Today, the insight unlocked by Dollar Shave Club has made them a mass brand. Successful mass brands always start out as a niche, because they always start small. But not just small—small and focused.

Dollar Shave Club understood its proposition. The people behind that brand worked hard to excavate the desires of the best customers to get to the problems they were really solving. Once they understood the real motivations, they added products to their offering and features to their user interface to turn those customer motivations into loyalty. Over time, that loyalty turned into referral, sharing the brand with like-minded people with the same motivations.

What they realized is that they were not selling razors [product] to millennial men [demographic]. The practical customers of Dollar Shave Club were paying for convenience and discovery. Products they needed or wanted to try were delivered, saving them a trip to the store and helped them avoid shopping. This gave them back time and provided them access to products and brands they would not have tried otherwise. Largely because the brands like Dr. Carver's and Wanderer are Dollar Shave Club private, house label that add to their own bottom line. Each time they added a product or category, it was positioned as a clever alternative to top selling brands.

What does specific even mean? For a niche brand like Stubble and Stache to grow beyond the nascent phase, the company will need to get specific with its customers. Is the product meeting the true needs of the best customer? As it stands today, they offer a really good beard moisturizer product. Do they understand what specific job their best customer feels he is solving? They cannot move from product to brand until they figure that out.

Assume the top purchaser of Stubble and Stache products are men. We can assume these men are practicing grooming, yes. But so many products would suit that need. Cheaper products with higher levels of awareness. What if the purchase rationale is more about achieving a level of refined self-care for a group that normally denies itself such luxuries? New products would have to be tested against such a goal to ensure they serve that same role, or a complementary one.

Not understanding their positioning would steer the brand towards bad investments, even without market testing. Assuming the brand is positioned as a shaving brand may lead to the idea of introducing razors to the product mix, à la Dollar Shave Club. This might have hit a small segment of their already small customer base, but it's not meeting the same need—it's not scratching the same itch in the customer's mind. But products like a moisturizing pomade or lip balm might.

MTailor is a technology solution to get consumers clothes that fit better. What's the specific approach to grow their brand? Again, you can assume the app provides convenience when it comes to clothes shopping. Pretty powerful. And that is half right. If you've ever shopped online for hard to size items, you will know the frustration of shipping items back. The app is not solving shopping, it is designed to prevent returns. That is something truly ownable.

Now the brand can organize around digital products and features focused on a more clear shopping experience that minimizes consumer confusion, product misunderstandings and returns. It can obviously align its physical product mix based on top selling items, styles and designers in its core categories. But they can tilt everything they do specifically towards being the online retailer that saves you from returns.

In *Disruption*, Jean-Marie Dru uses Tag Heuer as his famous example. The Tag Heuer watch campaign re-framed the way a luxury watch brand could talk about the importance of time by adding visually exaggerated stakes to time-based activities. A memorable campaign based on a now-proven theory: identify the way the category looks to consumers and do something radically different. The concept of specifics goes further.

In strategic planning, there are a variety of models for effectively communicating brand. A basic model is aligning the brand, the customer and the goals of both. While the theory described in *Disruption* and books like it sets a marketing layer over the top of this, it does not complete the circle. Yes, specific companies structure their marketing to differentiate the category norm—like Dollar Shave Club and Harry's. But they also expand the insights about the customer vertically within their entire company.

The entire category is moving in a particular way. Every competitive company is operating within the same playbook. How can your company play against that convention to truly separate? A niche brand has a foothold in the counter-current.

Is it possible to become specific by getting closer to a niche? Ben & Jerry's Ice Cream is another example of a brand that started as niche and it is hard to argue that it hasn't outgrown that label. The high-end ice cream brand was also acquired by Unilever (see a pattern?). Every move the brand made was aligning itself with its hippy ethos, from Grateful Dead themed flavors and responsible ingredient sourcing and selection to community involvement and causes. These were not merely marketing stunts or activations. The entire company is organized around the specific relationship between customers, employees, suppliers, products, distribution and beliefs, each piece carefully chosen to support and reinforce the others.

If another ice cream brand, say Blue Bell Creamery, wanted to claim this territory, it would start and likely end with marketing. This is no indictment of Blue Bell. As anybody who has ever worked inside one well knows, as companies grow, they become victims of their own structure. Established companies follow a path based on success and have trouble spotting new opportunities that lie beyond that plan. Or even the original opportunity that earned them their success. Sometimes they don't even see the direction a new player is taking until it is too late.

When an established company like Blue Bell identifies a new customer or market segment, it will follow a very predictable path. Hypothetically, Blue Bell may believe vegan ice cream is a trend worth investing in. The simplest thing to address is marketing. It is easy to create a campaign introducing the product line, explaining the reasons why their product is the best. But the product doesn't exist in a vacuum, does it? Blue Bell's brand is based on a theme of Americana, always referencing back to simpler times. Traditional American values. Baseball, amber waves of grain, apple pie, sitting under a shady tree with a Blue Bell ice cream cone on a summer day.

And not just subtle references. The advertising borders on Rockwellian, clinging so tightly to 1950's values that it is almost anachronistic. To launch a vegan product, the brand has to successfully walk the line between quaint Americana and veganism. The two concepts are not opposed but don't align naturally. They'll have to convince consumers that the all-American creamery understands the reasons that people choose veganism. They will also have to convince existing customers that the brand is still dedicated to its core beliefs, they cannot alienate the people buying today. Blue Bell customers will need to understand that current products haven't changed.

Can all of this be done? Of course. *Easily?* No.

Blue Bell has several advantages over a startup hoping to launch in this space. First, existing production equipment and facilities. Normally a huge head start over a new company. But in this case, special food and ingredient restrictions for vegan products mean that the Blue Bell production 'advantage' may be nullified.

They may need to find a partner, new production equipment or facilities—or even worse—build something entirely new. Meanwhile a company like Halo Top can start on day one engaging co-packers or building facilities that will meet standards for vegan food production or any other avenue they wish to pursue.

Next, distribution. All-commodity volume (ACV) is a powerful weapon an established brand uses to keep niche brands down. Blue Bell is available in thousands of retailers in the US. Let's assume their ACV is somewhere in the upper 80s. Remember the marketing launch that was so critical for consumers? There's an audience for the campaign that might be even more important. For new products, leveraging existing retail relationships to add product SKUs is a key to growth. Blue Bell will first have to convince buyers at retail partners and distributors that their new product will sell well, will make sense on the shelf, and will not cannibalize or diminish sales of other Blue Bell products.

Blue Bell has been so consistent and successful at building brand equity that it is now a prisoner of it. Again, a new entrant like Halo Top can waltz into the vegan ice cream category and convince consumers with vegan or other dietetic needs that they created their products *only for them*, not as an add on product to increase revenue. They can add customers without having to subtract anything. Everything they do is geared to building the bridge to that audience. They can focus on their one thing.

In this way a startup has an advantage over the bigger player, doesn't it? When Uber began investing in self-driving technology, Enterprise rental car bought Zipcar, a company offering convenient hourly car rentals. Enterprise was so focused on their path, renting cars and auto resale, that they missed the fact that they already had a fleet of cars that might have offered a competitive model to Uber and other rideshare brands. It may sound crazy, but one of Uber's biggest challenges to growth early on was getting enough drivers of well-equipped cars signed up to pick up passengers.

Here is the insight both brands saw that pushed them to make their respective moves. Auto ownership has been declining for a few years; especially in urban areas and especially with younger people. The same information brought Enterprise and Uber to surprisingly different conclusions.

Investing in Zipcar is a smart move if you believe people still want to drive a car they don't own (Enterprise). Or care about driving themselves at all. It is a crazy move if you think technology will continue to replace the number of cars people even drive. Each brand makes its money in a different way that gives their business its unique perspective and a moat that each is trying to protect. That perspective drove the decisions they've made. Enterprise, which makes money from fractional use of cars, saw the chance for further fractionalize usage—smaller parts. Uber profits from people hailing a ride. Which move is right? Time will tell. So far Zipcar customers have increased. A few years later, Uber launched

Rent, a service to let users rent cars, on their own, in place of securing a ride. Self-driving technology has yet to reach full government approval and meaningful adoption. The market will likely look different in five years.

Looking at Amazon, it is amazing that they can operate so many unique businesses from one central brain. But that's how they are different, one banner hosting dozens (hundreds?) of individual businesses inside, each chasing their own specific goal for their own specific customer. Amazon's single focus seems to be exploiting customer niches and growing them into viable businesses. Each can be small because they are supported by their dozens of sister companies, already bringing revenue to the hive.

MEME CULTURE

Mass media is not exactly disappearing, but it's certainly becoming more rare. Huge movies in the 80s and 90s meant that every person in the country had seen it (maybe more than once) and knew every beat of the movie. Hit television shows were watched by enormous audiences, and all at the same time. There was no DVR. Top 40 radio meant that there were 40 songs in a given week that every 18-34 year old American knew every word to or had Casey Kasem beat into their head.

Boo hoo. Those days are gone. We have a hundred times the number of TV channels and can create a custom radio station based on our every whim with a few clicks. This is not a sentimental walk down good old days drive. The point is, when we were all watching the same TV shows at the same time, we were all seeing the same ads. We were all subjected to the search for Herb at Burger King. We all watched in delight to see what the Bud frogs would do next. Wild times.

This not only limits reach from a media perspective, it shrinks the pool from which advertisers can draw references. Without mass radio, we all hear different songs and different sounds. There is still a Top 40, just heard by fewer people. Some of us never graduate to new sounds, still listening to music from high school. With fewer shared experiences, we have less common ground to draw from to bring audiences together. A recent TV ad for cinema ticket app Atom was based on a popular access using quotes from popular movies. The brand quoted the following films:

"I'll have what she's having." *When Harry Met Sally*, 1989
"Wax on, wax off." *The Karate Kid*, 1984
"Nobody puts Baby in a corner." *Dirty Dancing*, 1987
"Show me the money!" *Jerry Maguire*, 1996
"Yippee Ki-yay, motherfucker!" *Die Hard*, 1988

No film referenced was from later than 1990? It is possible that the target for the product is mobile users age 40-60, but why rule out younger viewers? At least part of the reason these quotes were chosen is because there are fewer quotes from more recent films that are as well known. There are fewer ways to quickly reference something a mass audience would understand as part of the cinema experience.

We are sharing fewer media experiences en masse. But we are still sharing media. At the very bottom of the scale are local, personal social media content seen and liked by a few hundred people in the network of the poster. This might be a baby photo on Instagram, a deep thought on Facebook or 'some personal news' on Twitter.

Above that are memes. Memes are a level of media and the secret nod among people in peer groups. Ask a new acquaintance "Do you even lift bro" and see if they get the joke or not. This is the same way people bond over movie quotes or song hooks. New movies are released weekly, new memes are born hourly or faster.

All memes are not squared up images with white Impact type or random Reddit humor. There are gifs, videos, tweets and fragments. Scenes from television shows and films get exploited or remixed. Pop songs are intercut or laid over dissonant video. Celebrities are roasted and exalted. Memes may be the last new media. Jokes, protests, ideas of all sorts are transmitted via meme. There are memes for all types of audiences. Funny memes, mean memes, wholesome memes, porn memes, absurd memes, sports memes, kids' memes and yes, dank memes.

Spend some time on *Know Your Meme* to see how fast memes are being born and spreading. The website has been chronicling memes and their spread since 2008. An interesting component to each meme documented on *KYM* is its origin. In almost every case, the researchers are able to track down an initial post. One post that appealed to a small group and grew. *Pool's Closed, Luigi, Slaps Roof, Slender Man*—can all be traced back to a single author appealing to a core audience who added to it and helped it grow.

Understanding meme culture is critical to understanding specific brands. Most memes do not expand past the first circle. Isn't this also true for brands? If you've studied your Ehrenberg-Bass you know that brands that grow have to reach the most people. But does that mean they have to be started with mass appeal? Most memes never achieve meme status but a very lucky few do.

This dynamic of something small and targeting becoming adopted into mass culture happens in all media and art. It is not exclusive to brands or memes. *Mean Girls* was a film released to low revenue expectations that became a hit, and shared by generations. It has transcended video and lines from the film are a part of pop-consciousness. Stop trying to make *fetch* happen.

Mean Girls is definitely not a movie for everyone. Like Tabasco isn't a flavor for everyone. The film is based on a book studying the behavioral dynamics of teen girls and written with a very particular point of view. The humor is off-beat compared to traditional broad American comedies. But it caught on. Partially because of its stars. Partially because it is quotable. Partially because the themes are so relatable.

Memes travel in the same way. *Slender Man* isn't a story very many people would have even seen based on its origin. The obscure story of a tall, featureless man who kidnaps kids *slowly* wormed its way into pop culture. The urban legend was created in 2009, in a Photoshop contest on the web community *Something Awful*. The story's origin is a grainy, relatively humble, image of a tall, faceless character walking behind some kids in a park setting. The rendering is indisputably creepy, and the lack of focus on the character in the image led people who saw it to begin adding their own ideas. And so they did. According to *Know Your Meme*, the character and the story quickly became too popular to contain on *Something Awful* and spread to other sites like Reddit and 4chan.

Like *Mean Girls*, *Slender Man* grew beyond the initial expectations, if there ever were any. Nobody in the mainstream knew the character for years. Why? It's surprisingly malleable. People were able to build on it and add their own chapters and characters. Views, mentions and new iterations of the story began to pile up when the video "Entry 1" was posted on YouTube by user Marble Hornets. Suddenly the character was dimensionalized and even more terrifying with the addition of a few new details.

As of 2018, a Google search of the words "Slender Man" brings up more than 90 million results. There are over 11 million videos, not including trailers for the major studio film that resulted from the character's popularity. The concept spread from nothing. Compare it to a well known brand that advertises. A search for Pillsbury, a brand that is over 100 years old brings up 270,000 video results. No surprise, most of these videos are produced by Pillsbury. They are mostly content marketing or ads. The content of these videos are recipes using Pillsbury products, or ads featuring the lovable Pillsbury Doughboy.

Number of videos is not a meaningful metric. In fact, Pillsbury generated millions of dollars while *Slender Man* was not a commercial endeavor for the first three years of its existence. Search volume for Pillsbury was double than for that of *Slender Man*, and higher still when Pillsbury was advertising, usually around the Thanksgiving and Christmas holidays, until a film was made in 2012. Even at this low volume of traffic, the story carried on and continued to grow beyond the most popular fanfiction and video.

The original *Slender Man* video by Marble Hornets has 6.5 million views. There are 27 others in the series with at least one million views. These are videos produced independently by the admirers of a Photoshop image. Of all of those Pillsbury videos available on YouTube, there are three with more than one million views. Recognize that those views were probably paid, and then realize that there was no paid media driving interest in Marble Hornets' homemade videos from 2009.

Is *Slender Man* a bigger brand than Pillsbury? Certainly not. Can *Slender Man* even be considered a brand? That's not the point. The point is that Pillsbury sells many products. In order to increase sales, they need to create mental availability for these products. Search volume tells us that when Pillsbury is advertising, they are more sought out. This is a combination of the ads effectiveness at creating need, and time of year. To do so, they spend millions per year. In 2017, they spent over $50 million, and over 40 of it in Q4.

Slender Man spent nothing. The story caught the attention of a small group who spread it voluntarily. Some created their own versions, details, characters and images based on it. There was nothing more to buy, but at least some would have. People observe culture and learn from it. As soon as we sit down as marketers, we observe other brands to learn from them. We miss opportunities to learn from the way messages travel especially when we focus on established brands that earned their position in a media model that is no longer possible.

Forget *Slender Man* for a moment. Replace it with one of the hundreds of other memes created every day. Each one of them builds in the same way. The right group of people finds the content and spreads it, adds to it, builds it. It is often perceived as useless or even unintelligible by outsiders, until it crosses a threshold that jumps it into pop culture.

Doesn't this also describe the way small brands start? They don't have mass market advertising budgets. They find a way to share their product or idea so a small group of people find it, spread it and build from a product into a brand.

There is a certain amount of content that gets posted online that never turns into a meme. It gets posted. It is barely noticed. It disappears. Memes, like brands, take many forms and are born on many platforms. When we talk about niche brands, you may think of those brands that are constantly popping up in your Instagram feed. Disruptive trousers. Cosmetics boxes. Nutrition shake delivery services.

Like memes, brands with potential have something worth talking about. And it is possible to do this incorrectly. When Peaches Monroee used the phrase 'on fleek' to describe her eyebrows on Vine in 2014, it caught on quickly. The phrase was widely repeated. And soon every mass brand in the world was describing their products as being 'on fleek' without any more context, and calling it relevance. Brands with the discipline to avoid jumping on every new piece of slang (or at least the restraint to do it in a clever way) rise above their desperate competitors. Brands that understand how to twist a bit of a meme into an ironic brand statement get even more attention and social credit with people in the know.

Several years ago, fashion brand Vetements gained international attention by 'designing' and featuring a DHL delivery t-shirt in their runway show. An ironic move already familiar to hipsters and thrift store aficionados vaulted the brand to success. For a while. When the joke faded, the brand followed. Meanwhile, Supreme avoids a similar outcome and remains a coveted brand with each product release (known to the initiated as a drop). Supreme maintains attention by doing periodic product drops with surprise items, some obvious (a sneaker crossover with Vans) and some curious (a hand axe). Supreme understands how to attract attention through interesting product selection and announcements, without crossing over into banality. The product mix and the drop is the marketing. The customers line up to get into a drop, and the community talks about the products they find the most interesting or surprising. Each of these conversations creates the potential for a Supreme brand meme on message boards or other places where fans of the brand communicate.

These examples are not repeating the story of traditional brands. It is 2019, and traditional brands are an endangered species. Looking at what has worked in the golden age can only take a brand so far. There is a new generation of media serving a new type of consumer, who is trained at birth to sniff out an ad. They would much rather spend time with the latest meme.

Specific : Adam Pierno

WHAT WE LOVE

Memes are fun but far from predictable. To understand how companies spread online, it is helpful to understand how music spreads. Music has always bonded humans. Musical artists created groups of fans that have proven to build powerful networks online. See: National anthems, football stadium chants, university fight songs and commercial jingles.

Also see: Pop music. As in memes, when songs or artists gain popularity, fans are proactively engaged and do the work on behalf of the band. Small gestures from the artist can catapult their work into the spotlight of mass culture.

The early internet was a series of gathering places for groups like music fans; people who collect around shared interests. Especially people interested in artists or music that is not widely popular. Growing up in the 90's, fans of Gwar were pretty isolated, unless they met others at their local record store. Today, you might be the only Juggalo in your high school, but just go to *Reddit* or Twitter and you have found your people.

People congregate and organize around artists, albums and styles of music. Brands would kill for that alone. In pop music there are wilder phenomenons. Go to Twitter and say something negative about Harry Styles. Watch what happens. Fans of pop stars organize their peers to buy, download and repeatedly listen to their favorite artists on streaming services, at key times, to help them move up higher in the pop charts. They mobilize around Soundcloud. They figure out the algorithm behind Spotify and YouTube recommendations and the Billboard charts. Remember the last time fans of your brand organized on their own for a week-long buying and promotion party? You wish.

In the early 2000's, people began reading about a legendary band with no name. The band played classic songs that no one could quite remember at a pub with no name, somewhere in Europe. There were posts on music bulletin boards, Ultimate Band List and Craigslist looking for records and bootlegs. There were suddenly people posting responses to the ads with links to mp3s of the sought after recordings. There were thousands of posts, shares, and downloads of the songs. Only, the band never existed. A team at JWT New York created the entire myth, and recorded the tracks. All to promote the Diageo brand Blackhaus.

What? Why? Because no one cared about the brand. It is a specialty spirit used only occasionally. But people did (and do) care about music. And they are entertained by a good myth (also known as a story). And a myth about music that tied to music and legends they *did* know was worth their attention, even if it was ultimately paid off with an ad.

What motivates music fans to act like this? What about music drives people to do this? Music touches people in a very specific way, it tickles something similar in the mind that is touched by memes. A combination of familiarity, curiosity triggers an emotion response. An actual emotional response. Doctors at Wake Forest Baptist Medical Center studied fMRIs of music lovers and found consistently that people's brains lit up when they were hearing songs they liked as opposed to when they heard music they didn't care for. Jonathan Burdette, M.D. noted that preferred songs of individual subjects had an impact on brain connectivity, especially on a brain circuit known to be involved in internally focused thought, empathy and self-awareness. The researchers also found that hearing favorite songs impacted connectivity between brain areas involved in audio recognition and regions responsible for memory and social emotion.

When Radiohead recognized their music was earning them less due to the limitations of their record contract and music piracy from fans using tools like BitTorrent, they hatched an untraditional plan. They posted their album *In Rainbows* on their own website, allowed people to download it and pay whatever amount they felt was fair. People could pay nothing if they chose. Did fans take advantage of the free music?

Yes, a lot of people downloaded the album and didn't pay, and the number of BitTorrent downloads was on pace with other new albums of the day. However, 3 million people also paid for the album, including almost 2 million copies on CD (remember those?) and over 100,000 special edition disc sets. *New Music Express* reported that Radiohead earned more from In Rainbows than they would have based on their prior record contract.

Why? The fans rose up. Radiohead's fans were so connected to the band's music that they opted to take action. Recorded music is a product. The band is a company and a brand that produces that recorded music. There is no documented brand statement. No pillars. Yet, music fans can provide a clear answer as to what they love about an artist. There is something specific that connects them to the music. It is a reason they downloaded the last album and why they will probably download the next one. An emotional bond exists. Most consumer products lack this.

Companies are full of people focused on, and fantastic at, nailing down details when it comes to the product. That is why employees may be tempted to say "our new vacuum has 8% stronger suction," or "this new furniture line comes in an all new blue color made from recycled pigments." Those details are important for sure. As a product description.

When Radiohead released the band's most recent album, there were a lot of questions. The band could have issued press releases that said "This album is 20% longer than our previous product," or "We used all new synth voices not yet created when we released our last product." They could have said "Johnny Greenwood played over 20,000 notes on this album," or "We're certain that Thom Yorke's voice proprietary to Radiohead and not available on the products of any of our competitors." But that would be absurd. Because none of those details would make a person more likely to buy the album. Or anything, really.

The average album release doesn't come accompanied with a fact sheet full of benefits and tech specs. In the case of *In Rainbows*, the band did have a product angle. The 'honor box' offering people to pay what they felt was fair which did make news and drew attention to the release. In most cases however, the fans figure out the pieces of information that are worth remembering or reporting. They choose the important stuff based on what strengthens the emotional connection, what they feel creates the social signals they want to give off (as only a detailed understanding of the production of a pop album might).

Artists—musical or otherwise—have a strong point of view. They are creating their first works to communicate something they feel inside or to simply share their point of view. It is specific to them. And they have a commercial incentive to produce something worth paying for. Later, some artists are able to craft artwork that will please their fan base (and yes, sell more).

Musicians know what resonates with fans from data most brands would pay anything to get: Live feedback. Performing for an audience allows them to see, hear and sense the reaction of the people in the room. The crowd stands and cheers for the song they have been waiting for. They go to the bathroom for the stuff they can do without.

For packaged products with no live feedback loop, this response is difficult to calculate. Instead there are a sea of metrics designed around the research that is currently possible. Consumers can articulate a response to a benefit. However, they find it difficult to explain a potential emotional reaction to a product, advertisement or experience they may face out in the world.

Examine romantic comedies, the movies we love to pretend we hate but actually love to love. Guess which film this describes: Two people meet. They are opposites. He's one way, she's the other. Though their first encounter puts them at odds they are thrown together by circumstance (a comedic one, no doubt). Slowly, over several scenes or (fingers crossed) a montage they observe something about one another that draws them in. They get close. Despite a spark, around minute 80 of the film, another circumstance (not comedic) threatens to separate them. But then at minute 88, fate overrides practicality and our couple decides they really do belong together.

Were you able to figure out which romantic comedy this is? *All of the romantic comedies made since 1980.* We all know that these movies follow a formula. Why? Because movie studios make products to sell for profit. The executives behind these movies want to create a predictable return on the investors' money. When they choose which films to invest in, they look at other similar films that they can compare against. This is where the fun and creativity stop.

To protect their investment, they conduct research using focus groups and other resources to get feedback on what has been created so far (maybe a script, storyboards, casting or even assembled film). The groups can not accurately predict financial results or performance. They can only respond based on things they have seen before. Inevitably, producers pull the film back to the mean. They change the story so that it has an ending like the endings of previous successful films in the category. They change the talent to be more like the actors in previous successful films. They repeat everything that has been done to ensure that they will be able to pull in a similar return. And sometimes they do.

They never deviate from the formula. They usually make a predictable amount of money in sales, some percentage of the one that came out last. People who love romantic comedies have a higher likelihood of seeing and liking the next one. But few newcomers fall in love with it, or the format. People who weren't convinced to see the last one aren't likely to come see this one. The audience does not really grow. Casual observers cannot tell one from another. Where does *You've Got Mail* end and *Sleepless in Seattle* begin?

True, your favorite movie might be a romantic comedy. If that is true, you can probably recite it line for line. You can remember the wardrobe the characters wore; the secondary actors who are now famous; the music from that montage when the characters realized just how much of a connection they had. You can remember the details the director put in the film (at least those that didn't get axed by the focus groups).

What creates the passionate response that makes a movie your favorite? Or makes you play a song on repeat? Or makes you share a meme? And what prevents most people from caring that much about a brand of soap or a restaurant? For 100 years, we've been thinking about brands pretty much one way, relying on a construct that is pushed through mass media. If mass media is changing (or at the least, getting less accessible) the construct needs an update.

DETAILS

If you have a favorite movie you can probably name the characters in that movie. The characters are probably *why* it is your favorite movie. You can recite their lines or recall facial expressions from the move. You know details about their behavior or back story. They almost always use music to fantastic effect. Not just a detail but an emotional one. These are the reasons you watched the movie a second time and told your friends they need to go see it.

In those movies you can't even remember what you saw. The characters don't stand out. They don't do anything remarkable. There are no details that mean anything to you. Here's the question: Did the details make you fall in love with the film, or do you remember the little things only because you love the film?

If you really think about it, the answer is *both*. Romantic comedies are an ideal example because they are rarely crafted by filmmaking auteurs. They aren't all known for the details. In fact, they are known to be devoid of details. And yet, the people who love them, still love them.

Now think about a pair of jeans you would never buy. Why? Something prevents you from choosing those jeans. Compare them to your favorites. The favorite pair fits a certain way. They have stitching that you love. The pockets are just the right depth for your phone. But more than that, it's the combination of details present and omitted that make the jeans feel like they were made just for you.

But I have already said people don't think about products. I meant, they don't think about products they don't love. And they don't love products they don't know. The details in how a brand is communicated (sometimes known as 'advertising') are what earn the attention which leads to trial.

This could be music in a video. Casting in a print ad. A filter on an Instagram post. A font. Details matter. Just as you are judging the quality of the thinking in this book by the details you observe, consumers judge the quality of a product by the lighting on the YouTube channel.

CONTEXT

There are some categories in which people have several preferred brands. As a coffee fanatic, I have lots of choices and exercise them based on context. This might mean emotional state, location, weather, and who I am with. If pressed, I would say Dunkin' makes my favorite cup of coffee. But that doesn't mean there aren't times that I choose, prefer or even crave another brand.

All each brand can do is produce a reliably similar product and experience so when a customer shows up, it satisfies the context that created the purchase.

Context also applies to a given retail environment. In the context of a brand's own store, people may find the product too expensive. For example, a piece of clothing. But when they find the same brand at an off-price or closeout retailer they may appreciate the same product as a value. At a department store, the Calvin Klein shirt is overpriced, ridiculous! But at Marshall's, it's a steal at 30% off. Clothing retailers incorporate this into their pricing and product strategy.

Change of context applies to food as well. When we see a new snack food in the grocery store we have one reaction to it. We may pass it by because the cart is already full of our regular chip brands, or we may be overloaded with options. Then we encounter the same snack at the checkout in a coffee shop and have a different reaction. "I've been meaning to give these a try." Why? The combined impressions created a new context.

Context applies to when we hear from a brand as well. If you listen to podcasts, you have been barraged with messages from direct-to-consumer brands like Meundies, Blue Apron and Quip. Hearing that same message has made it easy to ignore. But seeing a different version as a native video on a news site like Vox might make you more receptive, or at least attentive to the same message. New context, new potential.

Music and memes do not exist in campaign and non-campaign modalities. Maybe brands should not either. Brand and campaign modalities could be better viewed through context.

FACETS

There is a consumer drug that is advertised like crazy. It is used to treat plaque psoriasis. Made by Abbvie, the drug has been on the market since the early 2000s. The patent for the drug expired in 2016, and since then the brand has been airing on TV more than apology ads from Facebook.

There is another pharma brand that advertises just about as much. This one treats Crohn's disease and ulcerative colitis. The mild to severe variety. The drug promises control. Ads for this brand have been running since about the same time.

If you're an American, you won't be surprised to hear there is a third drug heavily marketed to consumers on TV. This one is sold to people who suffer from rheumatoid arthritis and promises remission. It has also been in the on-air rotation since that same time in 2016.

If you are expecting a chapter on competitive messaging and media, you will be disappointed. These three examples are *all the same drug*; Adalimumab, branded as Humira. Each illness has its own campaign. Its own creative. Its own tagline.

It is all the same drug. Same ingredients. Works in the same way. Luckily, the biologic has the effect of relieving all the above illnesses and more. What adalimumab actually does is a tiny reaction created at a cellular level. It binds to TNFa, reducing inflammation. The result of this gross oversimplification is reduction of symptoms of the conditions listed above. The control of each of these is a unique benefit to a different customer who is certainly searching for a solution. Amazing and rare.

Lots of consumer products do not have a single honest benefit (think soda). This one has a half dozen legitimate benefits. Instead of shoehorning them all into one sixty second ad, they have the good sense to break the top benefits into their own full campaigns.

Imagine the bravery it took to carve the brand into three distinct campaigns. Three times the planning. Three times the creative. Three times the media. Three times the cost.

Brands need to find the different angles that serve as entry points for new customers. Each benefit is served to consumers like the reflection of a funhouse mirror. Some reflections are improvements on our appearance, some are confusing. This is how we perceive product benefits. How does the product make us look? You know this question as the expressive benefit. It is a critical part of why we, as consumers, choose the products we choose.

Now imagine an entire house of mirrors in a fun house. Upon walking in, people are overwhelmed by images reflected back at themselves. In some, we look taller. In others, more squat. It is difficult to focus on a single image, when every move results in dozens of counter moves. There is no way for a person to register a single reflection.

This is the effect of the house of brands model. Maybe 'Badda book. Badda boom' is a memorable tagline, but I have no idea what brands it is connected to (or what it means). I have to Google it to find out that it is for the Choice Hotel lineup of brands. Unlike Humira, it can't articulate a meaningful proposition to a specific customer so it's lined up all its logos and paid them off with a nondescript alliteration. The message leaves viewers confused about who the hotels are meant to serve. As a consumer we expect a company to tell us why the benefits matter to me. What is the advantage of having the four hotels in one ad? What do I get out of it? How will it make me look? How will it make me feel? Who knows, I'm surrounded by reflections and totally confused. There isn't even an actual Choice Hotel in the Choice Hotels portfolio, just another dozen brands.

The urgency of the company to list its sub-brands, and parity benefits, clouds any clarity that reveals why a customer should choose them. Meanwhile, Abbvie has chosen a single reflection for each specific customer. It has clearly done its homework on the emotions and drive of that customer.

Clearly, pharma and hospitality are very, very different categories. They are different buyers and different buying processes. In both cases, there are many options for the respective target consumers of both companies. Humira has chosen to intelligently speak to each segment of their audience. Choice Hotels has chosen to beg anyone to book on their website. Picking on hotels is easy because it is so difficult to stand out, especially for mass market brands that have to win to the broadest audiences. These brands mistake mass reach for mass appeal, and put the pressure on the wrong elements.

Humira's end uses are an extreme example of brand facets. Each facet attracts a different specific customer, and no facet deters a specific customer from buying. Like a gemstone, each facet adds to the overall beauty and dimension of the brand, incorporating detail and context to complete the picture of the brand.

Facets complement each other in defining the brand for customers. They may create a tension but don't contradict or cancel one another. For example, some of Humira's facets are relief from individual afflictions. This doesn't contradict its efficacy with another affliction, but it may cause a tension for a consumer who is confused by a product that claims to treat both ailments that aren't known to be related. Another facet be its years of research and approval which causes no tension for the customer. The facets together define the brand.

A consumer may take in all the facets over time or may never explore beyond the facets that most appeal to them. To illustrate, let's look at a fictional paint brand. The company makes interior latex paints in a variety of finishes commonly found at hardware stores. In terms of quality and price it is in the middle of the pack. Based on other brands currently on the market, we can assume several facets of our brand.

Color. The brand has to first and foremost offer attractive colors that look current.
Coverage. The paint will have to be able to go far and reduce the amount of coats and labor.
Clean. The paint will need to be smudge and dirt resistant, able to stand up to household mess.

These are benefits, and not very special ones. For the category, they are basically table stakes. To become facets they have to be meaningfully connected to a specific customer: Who do we think will buy this paint, and who are we crafting the product and brand to attract?

The selection of colors on our paddle or wheel are critical to reaching this person. Is it high fashion colors that change with the season or tried-and-true colors that are comfortable choices to make? Do they like a 'safe' palette of colors with a premium offering of fashionable color accents? Even the format of the color paddle itself is indicative of the brand and help shape this facet. Is it a novel shape or clever fold? Is it printed on recycled materials?

When describing coverage, does this person want to buy less paint for price reasons? Do they want to do less work? Do they want to know the science or technical advantage to the paint that makes it superior, like the kind of additives that make it cover better? Are they just busy people who want to get the work done faster?

What does clean mean to this customer? Does he or she want to keep it clean from tough kids' messes like handprints and crayons? Do they just want it to resist minor dirt and smudges? Do they need to prevent commercial grade messes?

In this example, facets like color are not explicitly benefits. And they are not exactly what we describe as attributes. But they are something about the brand that connects to the target user in the way music does. A facet comes from both the product and the brand. It is not merely an advertising descriptor. A facet is a true story that connects the product, the brand and the customer. Humira really does address psoriasis. This fictional paint brand is really mixed in stylish colors. A benefit *could be drawn* from the facet of color. For example: an expressive benefit of having a stylish home.

Understanding the core customer means knowing the answers to each of the above questions and hundreds more. Each facet needs to be crafted for clear communication to the audience. What do they love? Why do they love it? How can the brand become something they love?

Specific : Adam Pierno

IDENTITY

Wait. We're all over the place here.
Memes, pharma, Radiohead, romcoms!
Where the hell are we going? All these
things are related. Everything created
for a commercial purpose has a brand.
A crap product you won't touch with a
ten foot pole has one of two problems:

A. It has a terrible brand.
B. It has a brand that is *designed
for someone else.*

I picked on romantic comedies earlier but all commercial movies today work the same way. We would like to get a certain audience to come to the theater; what would they pay to see? In the case of romantic comedies, the audience they are primarily created for is females. Then they adjust for age through casting, music and plot details. *Mama Mia* added Cher to the sequel—think they were trying to bring women under 24 into the theater? Seems like they realized Amanda Seyfried wasn't the draw for the core customer. A studio wants to remove as many barriers as possible to getting their target audience to go see it. Remember, the film is a product just like yours.

Marvel movies work the same way. Like *Iron Man?* Great, they'll put him in every movie. Even just for a few frames or a post-credits cameo. The people at Marvel have done their homework to figure out exactly which elements drive people to the theater, to buy Blu-Ray DVDs, toys, games, pajamas, etc.

Successful studios are very clear on their core customer. It all starts with the audience. The audience is central to the story, the characters, the casting and lest we forget – the marketing. If you spend any time browsing Netflix, you will notice how specific the offerings are getting. They are aimed at smaller and smaller initial audiences.

The most finely tuned brands understand their core customers just as thoroughly. They know their people very, very well. Who are the best customers? If the company knew 85% of their buyers would go away, who makes up the 15% of customers they would want to keep and build around? Those are their people. The brand needs to know the specifics that make those people tick and drive their daily decisions. That is just part of the equation. The data has never been more available. There are tons of companies that have all the data they could ever want and make great business decisions, but have no concern whatsoever about converting that info into a brand.

A brand is the result of shaping what the company does—what it is—around the best customer.

There are many producers of dog food. A walk down the aisles at a pet store will leave you bewildered if you've never done it before. And that is only a fraction of the companies that exist. A person with no dog would have a hard time listing dog food brands. That is the whole point. Awareness is great, but it is not exactly crucial that a person who will never buy the product have it.

Facets of a dog food brand involve ingredients, value, freshness, nutrition or easy digestion. None of those facets will matter to a person who does not own a dog. Facets crafted for someone with no pets would be a waste. The brand is shaped for the buyer first. In this case, the actual consumer of the product (yes, the dog!) is second.

So those facets have to appeal to the dog owner who might believe the dog will eat the food and get a benefit. But the facet does not have to appeal to the dog owner as the end user. For example, a focus on texture is wasted, since this person will never put the food in her mouth. In this case, flavor is often used as an ingredient cue, or as a point of reference, to decide if the dog will eat it or not—not as an enticement for the buyer, who will never taste it. They are not more likely to dig in to chicken, peanut butter or kangaroo because it is food for a dog. Instead, a focus on a shiny coat makes more sense because they can see a result.

The maker of a new dog food needs to know a lot about their customer. Normally understanding of levels of homeownership, top zip codes and leisure activities would yield a solid foundation. Demographics may not be very useful for a mass dog food brand because dog ownership crosses genders, ages and income levels.

There is a lot more information that can be used, more psychographics. At the top of the list might be how the person feels about their dogs. There is plenty to be extracted from this subject alone. Not specific enough. It would help to know some other details, right?

One area that is often overlooked is finding the other brands the core customer already uses. Identify the brands and work backward to understand why they may have selected each in its unique category.

Do people who buy organic dog food tend to be consumers of organic food? Do people who buy the lowest priced dog food tend to gravitate to lower prices everywhere? Do people who cook a lot tend to prefer fresh entrées for their dogs? Understanding these correlations would surely help shape the brand and make decisions around its development. A good guess for relevant index categories are food and grocery, home care and cosmetics and grooming. If they take care of themselves, they will be more likely to do so for their pets. It would also stand to reason that vitamins and nutrition is an important category.

Categories like dog food take more work to understand because there is no unintentional expressive benefit. When we choose eyeglasses, we think about how the glasses will make us look and what the logo on the arm says about us. That is the expressive benefit. In the case of dog food, a person can choose whichever brand they like and no one will really ever know. Want to feed them the cheapest food? Go for it. The purchase of dog food is a lot different from the purchase of jeans or headphones.

It is all customer perception and weighting of functional benefits. So the brands in the category tend to present a more logical case. They roughly stand for the same thing and present a similar argument.

MOTIVATING INSIGHT

That's not to say there is no emotional element. If you've had a pet you'll know there is. It can be very emotional. The brands that work the best make the most of the emotion. But real emotion is hard to come by. Most stick a tilt-shifted image of someone hugging a dog and call it emotional. It is not tapping into the root of the emotion. With all the information gathered about the core customer, the company can distill a motivating insight, a truth about the person's perspective on life. It is what drives them in relation to the category or problem they are trying to solve. The details of the person's life are meaningful but they are less meaningful to the brand than those that are about, in this case, dogs.

As the wisdom from Theodore Levitt goes, people don't want a drill, they want a hole. But that can be extended a step or two further, can't it? People don't want a hole, they want to anchor a piece of furniture into that hole so it doesn't get pulled over onto their toddler. That is zoomed in a little too close for the drill manufacturer to build an entire brand on, though.

The motivating insight finds the sweet spot between the product being sold and the reason they will buy it. For dog food, it is safe to assume most brands are operating off of a motivating insight about their core customer that says the person wants to give the dog a longer life to enjoy together. But it reads like an assumption written by someone trying to sell something.

A motivating insight that is useful for building a brand on has to encompass more than the basic benefit of the product. It has to explain a great challenge in their life they are working to solve or are driven by. It might capture a phase in their lives, not necessarily distilling their entire lifespan down to a pithy sentence.

A well-researched (and true) motivating insight becomes the foundation for the brand. For example, a motivating insight like "They feel a duty to take care of everyone in their life" provides a target to aim the brand at.

It seems a bit of a contradiction to say a broader insight leads to a more specific brand. In this case a wider view allows for a better way forward. A category insight makes nothing but category assumptions. There is no place for a brand to differentiate because it is only talking about the function and basics. A brand is not about a single product, or even a group of products. That is what a company is.

What can the brand do with the motivating insight? It can meet people halfway.

PROPOSITION

Now that we understand the person we are building our product for, we can shape the brand to them. How? It's called the brand proposition, the brand promise, the brand statement.

It is not a tagline. It is not a list of benefits. Classic marketing education dictates that a brand proposition be used to tie benefits together to create a unique selling proposition. It is rare for a product to have such unique qualities. What would make a dog food unique? In that category, the benefits are almost table stakes.

The best way to think about the brand proposition is something different. The brand is not talking to a specific person now, not a demographic segment, a zip code, or a generation (ugh). The brand will make them a promise. The proposition will be an oath. It must be a promise we are confident making and that we will be able to keep.

There are so many ways this can go. The promise is not pulled out of thin air. The goal is to build off of our strengths, the things the company does exceptionally well, and yes, the benefits to pay off the motivating insight of our best customer. We are promising Paul from Schenectady, NY, that we will do something which addresses his unique motivation as it relates to our category.

It should be clear now why the insight cannot be too close to the category. Going back to the dog food category, a motivating insight like "He wants to provide his dog a longer life" would yield 20 identical propositions from 40 different brands. All something similar to: "We help dogs live a longer, healthier life." There's no room to make this uniquely meaningful to this person.

The second insight we used, "They feel a duty to take care of everyone in their life" creates some opportunity for the brand. There are lots of ways the brand can connect to Paul based on this insight: He's a giver, he's generous, he's responsible, he values relationships, he understands that others' well-being enriches his own, he's not looking for the fastest way out. The promise should not be about the function, or the benefit to the dog. It should demonstrate support for his attitude toward taking care of people. Maybe a proposition like "Your dog counts on you and together we got this." "You do not always know what they need, but you know we do." "We will make you look as great as your dog thinks you are."

Notice two things about each option:

1. THEY ARE NOT TAGLINES.

A proposition should be easy to read, easy to remember and not use a single word more than is necessary. But it does not have to be a poem. It is meant to be *explicitly* understandable by the people working on the brand and *inherently* by all the Pauls out there, however they may encounter the brand. The brand proposition is not necessarily customer facing. Paul needs to get it, without ever seeing it in writing, because of how it is ultimately communicated and how the brand behaves in the world. This is a terribly difficult premise for marketing teams to do: write something and not buff it down to a shiny skeleton.

2. IT IS NOT FULL OF JARGON OR BENEFITS.

This may be even harder to avoid than attempts at a tagline. People feel safe when they see the word they feel is most important, or they believe their boss feels is important. They want benefits explicit in the promise. But in most cases, that yields parity among category competitors and lack of meaningful differentiation for Paul.

This work is important to building a brand, but it is rarely (if ever) done before there is actually a product, a service, staff, infrastructure. A company usually exists before the brand does, and certainly before the brand proposition. It is often the case that propositions fail because they can not be kept. The company would have to make changes that are difficult or expensive to make and keep that differentiating promise. Honesty is important, because the promise must be kept if the brand will succeed with its best customer.

WHAT YOU ARE NOT

Building a brand this way forces the company to decide what it is, who its best customer is and what its value to that person or people is. But in defining those facts, specificity allows something more liberating. Defining what the brand is *not*.

A valuable part of the brand architecture process is defining what the brand stands against. In sessions with brands of every size and stage of maturity, the answers fly when the moderator asks members of the brand team what the brand stands *for*. But on the inverse, the room usually falls silent. Beyond the clichés and corporate speak (We stand against boring! We stand against inefficient b-to-b data transmission!) comes the truth. Defining what the brand is against can give the brand and the best customer a common enemy which both are trying to avoid or eliminate. This also helps explain what the brand is not and provides a point of comparison for the desired customer.

Sometimes, what a brand is not can be more informative than what the brand is: "We are not the giant food conglomerate, we make handcrafted snacks. We are not preservatives and additives." "We are not beholden to legacy power and

manufacturing of vehicles. We are not stodgy or oil dependent."
Communicating to prospects what you are not is a powerful
way to define how the rest of your category falls short.

Better yet, it is a way to point out how the entire category
is the same, and can set up a conversation about how
you are different. And different is powerful when it aligns
with a motivating insight.

DISTINCTION AND SPECIFIC DIFFERENCE

People do not think a lot about how products are similar or
different until they have a reason to do so. They do not think
a lot about products in general. Building a brand on category
norms is flawed. Some things are expected when a consumer
buys a product. Toothpaste will have a minty flavor and leave
teeth cleaner, at the minimum.

There are times when it is not possible to have difference in a
product that is meaningful to the target customer. Changes in
sourcing and manufacturing have consumers of things from
toothbrushes to cars saying "They're all the same."

7Up, Sprite and Sierra Mist are essentially the same
beverage. As products they have no attributes that
consumers are likely to find distinctive. But they are
distinctive brands. Two have found specific methods to
make themselves distinctive from the others.

7Up has reformed its brand from the Uncola to the brand you
drink with music. They have pulled back from television and

focused on music, festivals and experiences that put them in front of consumers when they are enjoying their favorite artists or exploring new ones.

Sprite has remained on television, but aligned with the NBA. The brand has become distinctive by a decades long campaign using top talent in the league with high global reach. By sponsoring something its target customers love, in this case pro basketball, the brand has become different.

Sierra Mist has remained in a distant third place. It is the RC Cola of its category. Like RC, it failed to find a way to make its parity product distinct from its competition or meaningful to consumers.

Specific : Adam Pierno

FIT

It is one thing to 'craft' the brand proposition to your core customer, like a startup can. It is something else entirely to change your product or service midstream to reach them once it has launched.

Are Gillette's blades better or worse than Harry's? Who knows. It is a matter of preference, slightly less subjective than choosing a favorite color. It is easier for Gillette to write a new brand promise and a slew of new ads geared toward the customer they think is most likely to stick with them. It is much harder to go back to the drawing board and legitimately change the product. New Coke is a classic example of this. The Pepsi Challenge was winning share, so they changed the product. A huge risk.

Getting the product right from the beginning is the goal. And it rarely happens. Products launch with a goal, a target customer, a plan. Almost every company finds at some point they have to pivot sooner or later. Why?

Look at Twitch, the livestreaming juggernaut. Thousands of hours of video of gaming, vlogging, all manners of content are posted every hour. Users visit to see people play their favorite games; watching for ways to beat levels, earn achievements or just be entertained. It didn't start this way. Originally called JustinTV, the site meant to livestream people's mundane lives. Users carried or mounted cameras to share and document their everyday activity. Attending classes or going to the grocery store. It did not take long for JustinTV to fail.

Hardly anybody logged in to watch other people's boring activities. There was only one type of content drawing visitors - gaming videos. Twitch's founders figured out the core user and redesigned the product to delight users that were into video games. Then they started learning what other type of content this user liked best and built it out from there. Today Twitch is a huge success, purchased by Amazon, but they were almost out of business before they figured out how to thrive.

Physical products are a different challenge. Tooling, manufacturing and inventory have always put more pressure on companies because of the huge up-front investment and ongoing costs. It can take a long time for a company to see a return in the first place. If the product needs improvement, it can double that investment and the timeline for a return.

A kitchen cleaner with a trigger bottle that leaks can put a company under. A major design or assembly problem needs to be corrected, costing loads of time and money. A bottle for a specific customer who seeks a distinct, stylish shape or a unique spray pattern or intensity control can set a brand apart. But it likely has to be tested and tweaked before it hits. And how do you know what the customer wants inf the first place? A person in a focus group might say that he wants a bottle that grants more control, but in reality he picks the cheapest bottle on the shelf.

A consultant once told me a story about focus groups he observed for an electronics manufacturer. The company was testing designs for a new model of portable stereos (before iPods and the MP3 rendered all of this moot). They were sharing two designs with the consumer groups representing, made up of their target customers. One design that was in an all black plastic case; very nondescript and safe from a design perspective. The second design was in a brightly colored case, much flashier and different from anything on the market. The groups unanimously agreed that the brightly colored option was the better product. They told the moderator it would attract more attention, be more coveted and maybe perform better.

The researchers took careful note of the feedback. They put all the points on the board for the brightly colored version of the product. They discussed an increased price for the product to match the anticipated demand when it was released the next season. When they made their recommendation to the client it was a surprise: go with the nondescript, black version of the product. *Why?*

If you have ever conducted focus groups, you know there are some rituals. The participants get a meal before the group, usually sandwiches or fast food. The brand and consultants are behind a two-way mirror, and usually devouring M&Ms. The moderator always—Always!—has a pre-set series of corny jokes they use before every group.

At the end of most focus groups, the moderator usually reveals the company sponsoring the research, if it is a consumer brand. And the brand usually offers the participants a coupon or a sample of the product. In this case, the company provided two tables of brand new portable stereos, the very same they had just been discussing. Not sure which they would want, the company provided equal numbers of each version. As the participants left the research facility, each chose a stereo. The table was left with only brightly colored personal stereos sitting on it. The consumers had revealed their true preference. The exact opposite of what they had been saying for the prior hour.

People are not good forecasters of their own behavior or decision-making. Most of us do not understand why we do the things we do well enough to guess what we will do in the future, even the near future. This is a flaw in consumer research which asks people open ended questions about their future self and provides little guidance or context. To get a product right, people have to understand the context, the detail and the benefits that would be valuable—sometimes, these are features and benefits that do not yet exist.

In-home user testing is a much better predictor of feature adoption because the person can rely on much more context to understand the benefit and potential value. In a focus group or online survey, it is difficult for any person to guess how much better an ergonomically designed switch will be.

Product has to be built around the specific problem you are trying to solve. The specific task you are trying to do better. The specific person who will value what it is. Therefore, every decision, every material, every curve, every pixel has to be assessed through that single prism. Will this make our product more valuable to our customer?

At this exact moment, you are dreading an anecdote about Apple's commitment to product. Relax, it is not coming. It has been covered to death. Instead, think about brands that have truly understood their core customer and made changes that their specific customer would view as improvements.

Nintendo, once the dominant player in the home gaming market, is now a solid third-place entrant. What they do well with each upgraded system is find one innovation that creates space for its games and reminds core fans what they love about it. In 2006, sensing they were losing ground in the open world and first person shooter territories, they introduced Wii. The system had a novel controller that captured full body movement along with traditional push buttons.

The novelty faded after Nintendo struggled to release games that capture the original challenge of the Wii system and Microsoft added Kinect interactive functionality to Xbox. Wii showed Nintendo where their blue ocean is. The success of the Wii was never going to be shooting games for hardcore gamers; no, it was the family system. Sure it had standard franchises like *Madden* and *Call of Duty*, but games like Wii Sports were picked up by families who turned the game into lively challenges. A father would usually squash his young daughter in a tennis match, but not so in *Wii Tennis*. She had a fighting chance and it was fun.

Their next system, Switch, incorporated the lessons of the Wii and added new features to please that customer. They kept the active controller style, but doubled down on the activity potential by making them smaller and lighter and adding some extra haptic effects. They also made adjustments to the design so controllers can be assembled into something more closely resembling the larger controllers of Xbox and PlayStation. Kids who grew up with Wii still had games that used movement, but could now explore games popular on other platforms in a more familiar way. Parents can add additional controllers to the console and most games allow fun multi-player modes for this family audience.

They also incorporated a portable touch screen into the dock and controllers that latch onto either side. This allows the game to be portable and feel like an expanded mobile device. This lets the game go on car trips or to waiting rooms. They kept game cartridges, but added online games that can be downloaded to the console like customers have gotten accustomed to on the App Store or Google Play.

Finally, the games. Nintendo delivered their core characters (the ones mom and dad grew up with) in ways that felt fresh but also fun. *Super Mario Odyssey, Donkey Kong Country, Kirby Star Allies, Mario Kart 8* all play best when multiple generations are playing together. Older players are instantly familiar with the characters, which makes learning the new styles of play fun.

Monzo has figured out an insight about banking customers: roughly 99% of them don't like banks. We forget that banks were once tied to local communities. The local bank knew the people in the neighborhood, helped them buy homes, save for college, build businesses. Technology made banks so big there is barely any human contact or empathy for most banking customers today. Monzo built their service and products to reach the customer looking for community and to rebuild trust. They speak in plain words (must have read *Under Think It*) and are very clear at all points of communication, unlike most banks.

They have also put technology first, but in a very friendly way that makes the brand feel much more accessible and transparent. Like Uber, Monzo is focused on a slick and friction-free user experience. They had features like peer-to-peer lending and check splitting early on. Monzo has launched with no branches, relying on their app to break through with customers. Their platform is seen as highly intuitive and comfortable to use. Most banks, even when trying their hardest, come across as opaque and challenging to deal with. Monzo shares issues they are working to solve and asks for feedback before acting—and genuinely appears to consider the feedback they get. When their original name was lost to a trademark challenge, they turned to their community to help them come up with the name Monzo.

In 2017, they announced to customers that they were facing rising fees for international ATM withdrawal access and were considering how best to cover costs while limiting customer fees. They actually gathered feedback, shared multiple proposals for a new policy on the matter, then allowed a vote. Then they openly shared the result. As a kicker, the resulting policy seems pretty fair to me as an outsider. The company didn't try to turn fees into a profit center, only to cover their exposure.

They did three things extremely well which demonstrate a specific understanding of their customer. First, they explained to the customer that they had a business problem that needed to be solved. Most banks—wait, no banks—handle customer communications this way. They would explain the fee with an email after deciding on the course of action.

Next they asked for feedback and actually listened. It is clear from the content on their website that they really did listen and continue discussing the options and ideas with customers as well as bringing customer ideas back inside the Monzo offices for further review.

Finally, they gave a detailed explanation of what they chose, why they chose it and what it would mean to customers. They also took the time to acknowledge that not all customers selected the option they took and apologized. Can you imagine?

Many banking customers are disillusioned with the entire category, resigned to give away a percentage of their money in fees for the privilege of storing it. Monzo capitalizes on that by showing a friendly face and living up to it at every touchpoint. They limit fees and explain them clearly to keep up the trust the customer has been missing all along.

Monzo flies in the face of stuffy bank brands not with glib ads, but by doing things like keeping a running list of things they want to improve and asking customers to follow along with their progress in real time. When has your bank done anything like this? Their challenge: most people don't want to change banks, and most consumers trust the banking system (despite loathing it). The Monzo customer has a sense of adventure and is willing to try.

Some brands get it, but then lose touch with the specific customers that helped them grow over time. Playboy was born in an era when gender roles were much, much different. In between well-written articles were artful nudes of women posing on tennis courts, riding horses and bathing. The racy publication never quite crossed the threshold into pornography like its rival print publications of the 70s and 80s. But it was always clear, even in the masthead, that *Playboy Magazine* was intended to be "Entertainment for Men." They spent 50 years burnishing that relationship with their male target audience through interviews, articles and, yes, bare breasts.

Beginning in the 1990s, things changed. There is no question that the brand's place and meaning in US culture was shaken and usurped by the combination of lad magazines like *Maxim*, *FHM* and *Loaded* full of girly magazine pictorials on one side and freely available pornography via the internet on the other. Playboy had cultivated the image of a sophisticated men's brand with an intelligent point of view. Stuck in between dumbed down and filthy versions of its top performing content, the brand had become irrelevant to men.

Suddenly, in the early 2000's the brand was back. But not in the way we knew it. Instead of rising up online or on its licensed pay-TV channels Playboy showed up on E!. A new series called *The Girls Next Door* depicted the odd four-way relationship between Playboy founder Hugh Hefner and his three girlfriends living in the Playboy mansion.

Playboy was cool again. But not in the same way and not with the same specific audience. Instead of being read by men, the brand was now a hit with women. Licensed products with the signature bunny logo started popping up everywhere but not among men. This time it was women and girls identifying with the fun playmates of the E! series and the idea of female empowerment.

As women adopted the logo as their own symbol of confidence and sexuality, interest among men waned further. The print publication was relegated to being a loss leader; its new purpose was reinforcing Hefner's legacy and supporting higher revenue merchandise sales. The brand became part of broader pop culture, but the intelligence of the brand was distorted by a crass sheen due to the TV show. Men, with many options for content and confused by the new iteration of the brand, left and didn't come back.

When the odd relationship(s) between the three Playmates and Hefner finally dissolved so did the cable show. And so did the brand. Once unmoored from its heritage, the brand no longer connected with men. Once the short-lived E! series disappeared, the women who adopted the brand moved on to the next fun trend. It took years to re-establish itself in the US after several stalled relaunches.

Peloton is another brand that understands its customer and advantage. This is in part because the company was founded by people looking for a solution to their own problem. A group of cyclists wanted to find better workouts and had trouble doing it on a convenient schedule. They looked to technology to help, by putting the best instructors on a screen attached directly to the stationary bike.

Coming from a place of solving the problem, they created the solution they craved. Their offering, an expensive bike and an ongoing subscription costing four-times that of Netflix, appealed to a specific consumer. Not only the fitness obsessed, but those with the means to invest in it.

There are more than a dozen classes live-streamed daily to create the kind of convenience that wasn't offered at in-person studios. Can't make one of those? Pull from a library of thousands of past classes. As riders pedal through a class, their progress and stats are displayed on the touchscreen in real time. It is expensive, but to the customers who can afford it, the workouts and control are worth it.

Peloton has been described as a hardware company, a software company, a fitness company and a cult. While spin enthusiasts are a devoted lot, Peloton riders ("spin" is trademarked) take it to the next level. They do multiple workouts per day and make pilgrimages to Peloton studios for live workouts.

There are a lot of people who love cycling or spin. Peloton might have chosen to launch a gym. Instead they capitalized on the insight that people who want more control of their workout schedule may want more control over all aspects of their workout. They can choose the instructor, type of workout and the exact start time. By providing that control and more, Peloton has been able to charge a premium, which reinforces the brand as a luxury for the truly dedicated, as opposed to inviting comparisons to a gym membership.

How many other brands exist for fitness? Hundreds? Thousands? They range from gym and clubs (Planet Fitness, 24-Hour Fitness) to large equipment (NordicTrack, Bowflex) to smaller items like AbDoer and Shake Weight. They are all offering the ability to exercise on your time and in the way you want. Trend and technology came together at the perfect time to allow Peloton to offer this type of control over a workouts for a very particular customer.

JP Morgan Chase & Co. figured out a simple way to stand apart from all of the competitive credit cards with their Sapphire Reserve card. Not by addressing interest rates; that had been going on for years. They did offer aggressive bonuses for new accounts in the form of rewards and frequent flyer points, which didn't go unnoticed. More importantly though, they became more immediately distinctive by feel and weight.

Forever, or at least since the 1960s when credit cards were introduced, they have been referred to as the slang 'plastic.' Every card from Diner's Club to American Express Platinum have been made of the same substrate, with account numbers stamped in the same way, 20 percent of the height from the bottom.

Chase identified a weird gap in the marketplace, one that hadn't been successfully leveraged before. Why are all cards made of the same plastic? They made their premium card from metal. The Sapphire Reserve card stood out immediately with a unique texture and heft. Immediately, users recognized this new card was different from the other cards they had before. The card was easier for customers to identify in their wallet by feel. The metal substrate was cooler (in temperature and to some, in style) and easier for the thumb to stop on. The novel material made the card an objet d'art – fun to show off and for customers to put on display. In group settings, when friends offer cards for the bill after a meal or drinks, the card became a conversation piece, landing on the table with a 'clink' instead of a 'tap.'

The gap that Chase found in the marketplace didn't relate to the user, just to the material. Yes, they offered aggressive incentives for new customers. That is semi-standard in the credit game. Especially for the high-income, premium customers Chase was seeking. Chase identified a way to reach them that was truly distinctive and design based. In retrospect, it was obvious.

Why hadn't anyone tried this before? Because conventions are powerful. Credit cards have always been plastic, and so credit cards are always plastic. This is how they're made, so this is how we make them. Chase stood up with a bold approach to change the way consumers view credit cards. Since then, Master Card has launched a Black Card made from a stainless steel veneer over a carbon fiber body. Effects are still to be determined.

In each of the positive examples there is a clear departure from trying to be for everyone towards being for someone specific. These are key uses that the company determined would create preference and loyalty. Peloton chose to focus on producing the class content that drives daily—or multiple times daily—interest amongst core customers. Though the bike hardware itself gets great reviews from customers, it doesn't create the fanatical following of Peloton riders alone. The video content, and its integration into the riders' experience, is what keeps people coming back to the bike.

The initial cost of the Peloton bikes along with the set-up process are meant to create a commitment to the product that serves as a lock in of sorts. Instead of merely unboxing the bike and riding, the bike requires a scheduled installation by a representative of Peloton. This installation is a bit of a pain, but is an immediate demonstration of the difference between Peloton and other home exercise products. Most other home fitness can be ordered on Amazon and delivered by anyone. It's set up by the owner.

This discerning fitness customer wants to know they are getting into something supercharged. Most likely, they are used to high-end class experiences and are reluctant to trade those for an at-home workout. They want to know setting up Peloton is worth their time. That it requires installation at all differentiates it in the mind of this customer, and the nature of the installation ensures the customer is shown all of the features that make it special. The installation is part demonstration, part education. They are now part of a community. Each Peloton rider, a member initiated through the rite of installation.

Being specific is all about making space for the brand. Nintendo continues to break ground with a series of homegrown innovations that carry from generation to generation. They designed their Switch system not to compete with the heavyweight platforms. By design, the Switch has less processing power and slower refresh speed. Nintendo made a strategic bet on a gaming space between mobile phone-based gaming and games found on Sony and Microsoft products.

The Nintendo Switch is light-weight, literally and figuratively. It's designed so a novice gamer can sit down (or jump around) and figure out how to play and how to play with their kids. It's designed to be an antidote to heavier, violent, higher commitment games that take dozens of hours to beat. That the entire system can be undocked and carried to another room, or another place without ever being paused, suggests Nintendo had in mind an entirely unique use-case .

Both Nintendo and Peloton planted facets that their core fans could latch on to. The Switch has enough Easter eggs tucked in the game to keep older players engaged. Like Iron Man appearing for just a few frames in the next Marvel film, finding a two-dimensional board from the original *Super Mario Brothers* inside a board on *Mario Odyssey* is a hook that makes young players ask "What is this?" while older players tweet their surprise at the discovery.

It is not because it's a super challenging piece of game play or because it competes with *Far Cry*. It is because to this person, finding details like these create interest and drive more game play. Every time a rider finds a new instructor or killer workout on their Peloton, they start thinking about their next ride. They tell someone else. They become more loyal.

These products have been designed with a motivating insight in mind. The Nintendo Switch offers freedom and flexibility. Xbox and Playstation platforms are designed primarily for a single player to control the deck. Games are focused first on single-player mode. They come with one controller. It is all about centering a person in front of the console, in front of a television. Everything about the Switch's design is about being untethered. The game can be played without a television. It can be carried around or transported to wherever a player goes. The controllers can detach, attach, or be used in a variety of configurations. A parent probably doesn't have to worry about the content of most of the games. It's more powerful than mobile games and more portable than hardcore games. It is designed to be configurable to handle the preferences of multiple people in more places and used in more ways.

Peloton also provides control at every turn. The user of this product would probably be considered a little obsessive about their routine. Peloton has a designed a system based on choice and fine-tuned control. It is quality hardware combined with quality content in a novel format (at least when introduced). Even now as NordicTrack and others launch their competitive products, they're not going to steal this specific customer. The details about Peloton appeal to the Peloton customer, who is not a price-driven customer. Peloton is positioned around social status so the new challenge is finding more customers who can afford the brand without losing the prestige they've created.

Remember *Slender Man*? It spread because it appealed to a core audience who could build on it. Monzo bank customers are looking for a clear picture of their finances. The app is designed to be a killer user experience that provides simple visibility and no fees. Features that allow a user to simply send money to others helped the app go viral. It was baked into the bank's app before most other banks had their own proprietary sharing feature. Each person who received money from a Monzo user was greeted by a message introducing them to Monzo, and of course a note from their friend. Monzo offered the service for no fee, encouraging more users to share with more friends.

Peloton allows users to track and share results. Great, other Peloton users can see the results? No, even better. Peloton workouts can be shared directly from the touchscreen to a variety of widely used fitness apps or wearables like Strava and Fitbit. Users of these apps see a notification by someone stepping up their workout frequency, performance and most likely their accompanying comments. They want to know why. The answer is Peloton.

Nintendo enabled the Switch to play in online mode that encourages people to invite their friends. 'Don't have a Switch? Get one so we can play *Super Smash Bros*!' The game play is fine for one person, or a group, but even better when more people are added remotely. The Switch console can link with other Switches that are connected to the same Wi-Fi network to encourage all new types of multiplayer games.

As you can see, each product is sharpened with a specific person in mind. Each fork in the road allowed the company to steer in the direction that customer would choose. The best products are a demonstration of understanding, a love letter to the customer they serve. For Peloton, it is offering more ways to put the rider in control of their workouts. Chase designed its card to reach people seeking a visible sign of status. For Switch, it means finding more and more ways to untether the gamer from a seat on the couch. For Monzo, it means a simpler way to manage money for those willing to trust a new banking model.

The product is shaped to satisfy the motivating insight. By satisfying that motivation, the brand builds affinity. Through that affinity and usage, the customer uncovers more things to love. Those items create loyalty and more discovery. Finally, the details of the product encourage the user to share the product with others who share their motivation. The product designed for someone so specific builds a following of customers similar to the original customer, even if they'll only use one feature.

A Peloton rider doesn't need to use every bell and whistle built into the system. She might find an instructor on her first ride and never look for another instructor, but still be a happy customer. She might share on the mobile fitness app Strava, or might never have heard of Strava, and can still love the product. In some cases, just a single feature designed so well creates the impetus to share with others. The brand provides facets that thrill the specific customer.

Specific : Adam Pierno

ELE-MENTS

To say that a product is created for someone specific means that each choice is selected for that person.

For example, the smaller size of the Nintendo Switch controllers are deliberately designed to better fit the hands of children. We make choices to better suit, better fit and better appeal to our specific customer, or we risk market place confusion. The temptation is to design products that appeal to all. Products that don't turn everybody off. That approach tends to create products that fail to fascinate *anybody*.

People understand and appreciate something that is designed just for them. This is how product or brand loyalty is born. Your bits of plastic fit my hand better than your competitor's bits of plastic. The spray nozzle on your product is at an angle preferred over your competitor's. The font and colors you chose appeals to me. Or you could choose pre-existing tools and pieces and go to market with the same handle or spray bottle as every other product on the market. No one might object to it, but will anyone love it?

There is a secondary effect to specific design. The next ring of potential customers may not love the details. But they will recognize that there were details selected for a reason. They will understand the company has created a product for a purpose. *It is angled this way to better achieve this purpose.* They may not have had that specific problem, but they can appreciate that the company is offering something beyond a generic solution. They mark this company because it has a point of view. The company is now a brand.

Method came out of nowhere in the early 2000s to win miles of shelf space in the home care category. Before they launched their first product, package design was essentially generic. They entered the market with that understanding. Giant product companies had refined their categories to the bare essential and were delivering products Americans had been buying for more than 50 years.

Method's founders saw the opportunity to disrupt by serving what was then considered a niche: people looking for more natural ingredients and new approaches to cleaning. They also understood that consumers would perceive the difference in ingredients if the packaging also stood out from the Procter & Gamble and Clorox mainstays that had dominated grocery shelves for so long. They offered sleek packaging that looked more like art than containers and dispensers. Why?

The packaging was an immediate signal to people looking for new solutions. They had never seen products like these on the shelf, and suddenly Method was there to fill a gap they hadn't ever known they were seeking. A clearly different product for a different customer than the traditional buyer of consumer packaged goods. Traditionally, Clorox and Procter & Gamble's product design was utilitarian, white spray bottles with standard triggers, a foil coated cardboard cylinder. The Method design aesthetic was a combination of sleek, ergonomic curves creating products their customers wanted to display in their homes instead of hide in cabinets.

Even people who weren't looking for more natural ingredients noticed the packaging. And people who weren't moved by the packaging still registered the product differentiation from the Procter & Gamble lineup. The design made the company a brand. Instead of selling a product, Method launched by selling a difference. Both a visible, tangible difference and conceptual difference. They had an immediate point of view that invited some people in, and gave others an opportunity to decline the invitation.

Brands are greater than products. Go to the hardware store and shop for screws. You might ask 'What kind of screws?' The answer would be a purpose and perhaps a material. Screws are all designed for a purpose. There is a correct material for each purpose, depending on what is being connected. Some are made from steel or alloys and coated for appearance or support. So there are five potential questions to help define the correct type of screw. Screws are products or mere companies.

Not one of those questions is "Which brand?" Screws have not been designed for a person. Depending on the hardware store you choose, there will be a different set of manufacturers' screws, or perhaps a single one. Why? At fractions of a cent per unit, the investment in a brand won't quickly pay off. At a sales level, the vast majority of screws are sold to builders in bulk. They are fired into wood or metal and then taped over or otherwise hidden. If the structure stays up, the screw is forgotten forever.

Individual product design is essentially locked. There are new types of screw heads created about every 25 years, and adoption of tools controls new entrants there. Automakers and other manufacturers adopted the Torx or star head screws to prevent tampering. Slowly, people adapted by purchasing the drivers. Material is going to be part of the commoditization of the category that hasn't been upended. Unlike Method's approach, there is no demand for alternate 'ingredients' or means of production in screws.

The packaging is also lacking the opportunity for a benefit. Most packaging is a box or plastic case with a simple sticker or label. Not much going on. Serving a dual purpose of storage and stability, the packaging has to hold hundreds of screws and not tip over in a work environment. An innovation in package design would have to make the product easier to grab, less likely to roll over and make working with them faster or better somehow. And it would have to offer a meaningful advantage, without adding significant costs. Because screws are a commodity, after all.

Let's go back up a level.

Which store did you think of? Before this fascinating digression about screws, you conjured a picture in your mind of walking through the aisle of a specific store just by me naming the category. That's not an accident. Depending on where you live, the stores nearby are designed for you. The logo has been designed or modified *for you*. The color and shape of the staff aprons and uniforms have been selected for you. Which brand is orange, blue, red?

The width of the aisles has been considered, along with the footprint of the store. When you walk into an Ace Hardware, you have a sense of where you'll find screws, if you've ever been there before. Have you ever noticed that the impulse items at each hardware store is different? At smaller stores, there are more small tools and items. At big box stores there are more snacks and batteries. Lowe's checkouts are getting merchandised more like a traditional convenience store. Refrigerators holding a variety of beverages, lots of bags of chips. Meal replacements.

Every part has been considered for the shopper. The shopper they know is more likely to choose their store over the competitors. These choices are designed to make the product more enjoyable, lead the customer down a particular path (sometimes a faster one), and to ultimately sell more products.

Software designers are focused on UX, but they have nothing on retailers. They are using the same personas to design similar flows. Conversion pathways. Retailers even design dark patterns to keep shoppers in designated flows; something commonly attributed to software design. It is all just happening in physical environments instead of inside an electronic device.

Retailers are not always incented to provide the fastest or smoothest experience. They're designing their stores to fulfill the experiences that customers expect. For some brands the most fulfilling experience includes discovery. For others it is just about speed; get customers in and out. Some stores are set up to add products to your basket by putting complementary product near each other. Some are set up to sell more expensive items by anchoring prices.

They are laying out a planogram of each section of the store to make it as effective as possible at getting to the consumer and meeting them at their motivating insight. Some retail brands thrive on sensory overload, cramming as much merchandise in per square foot as possible. Think Best Buy or Bed Bath & Beyond. Those retailers understand that those shoppers come with a short shopping list. They change aisle heights, widths and shapes throughout the store, creating a visual challenge that makes it difficult for consumers to compare products and prices. The store design is set up to offer potential visual cues to the consumer that will prompt add-on purchases.

Other stores are designed to be precious and spare. Think high-end boutiques and jewelry stores. They are not overly merchandised. Empty space is a show of luxury. They are making a demonstration of the importance of each item. This necklace is so valuable, we've surrounded it with nine square feet of empty space that we pay for every month. Excess space is a hallmark of luxury branding.

This same rationale explains why drug stores include one of every bottle of perfume it carries in its print ads. The media space is too valuable to the store to waste a pixel. They need every square inch to be returning revenue. They demonstrate an excess of options, as if hoping you will think "Whatever I need is there." But fashion ads show one tiny image over an entire page of black ink, next to an image of a model. The space around the product indicates it's preciousness, deserving of its own air.

The environmental design both satisfies the needs of the intended shopper while defining the experience for that person. In the drug store, for example, the store is packed with low-cost items. This design is transactional. The intended shopper finds the items they need and goes. The store layout says *you are meant to come here to satisfy requirements; to cross things off your list.* But in the luxury store environment, the experience is focused on the experience itself. It is meant to be posted on Instagram. The shoppers are meant to have a different point of view when they leave the store.

In a luxury retail environment, white space creates the opportunity for the shopper to reflect upon the item. It demands focus. No product is more aware of distribution of product per foot than auto dealers. Go to a used car dealer and examine the lot. Every corner of the property contains a parked car. They are hoping to maximize sales per foot, and suggesting to the customer that there is definitely an option on the lot for them. It is a giant grab bag of cars. Cars made for a wide variety of audiences. The used car dealership does not make choices to suit a specific buyer.

Compare that to a Mercedes-Benz dealer. They know exactly who is coming in. The prices of those cars is well-known, and dictates a relatively wealthy customer.

Again, consider how high end dealerships use space. The interiors of these dealerships have a luxury aesthetic as it relates to space. They waste it. It is all a show. It looks like an art gallery. Hmm. That would make the vehicles art, now wouldn't it? Too precious to be packed in with other cars. Luxury car brands invite customers to sit and think about it with a cup of coffee or water. "How lucky am I to be here at the dealership about to drive off in a Maserati?" The cars are visible from every angle as if to tell customers "There is nothing to hide. This is no trick. This car is as beautiful as you think."

And of course the experience design of the sales staff. Go to a traditional used car lot or economy brand and the sales staff is walking briskly towards the customer before they exit their own car. At luxury dealers the sales staff remains at a distance, waiting patiently. They often speak in hushed tones to remind you there is no pressure. "There is nothing to pressure you into. This car is available only to those fortunate enough to afford it. If you are deserving, it can be yours."

Cars themselves are a perfect way to look at specific design. There are some basic elements that have become convention in the automotive space. There is so much room for design decisions that will present facets and connect with the specific audience the car was made for.

The customer at that Mercedes-Benz dealer is looking for luxury. They enter the car looking for affirmations that the car is worth the price and delivers on their expectations. Someone shopping for a Ram truck is not starting with the cockpit. The towing power, cargo bed and performance come first. They have a different criteria.

When we shop, we are subconsciously asking ourselves "Is this the one I'm supposed to choose?" We look for signals. It is evolutionary. Is this a mark of my tribe? Is this a safe place for me? The brands that succeed have decoded the signals and make sure we receive them.

Each brand or make is made up of a set of signals that invite or reject potential buyers. Even within a single brand think of the different shapes of the driver's compartments. The height and slope of the dashboard. The amount of glass, or wood or plastic. Display screens.

First, the seats. When a new car buyer enters the car they will press against the driver's seat. Their hand and arm will run across the material to lever their body in. The look and feel of that seat is a critical first impression of the craftsmanship. Is it soft or stiff? Will it be easy to clean?

A parent buying an SUV will have a different focus than a single woman buying her first car. The parent wants to know if it can seat her children, plus a friend or two if needed. That the car won't look like a war zone after two weeks of carpools and snacks. That there is storage in the cargo compartment. She may look for plugs and entertainment. She may look for a vacuum. The back seats become more important than the driver's area.

The details of the seats themselves identify the buyer. Are the seats styled with multiple colors and textures? Is there detailed stitching? These are signals that make the car feel more custom and luxe. Some customers will insist on real leather or even a type of leather. Others will settle for something close to leather.

For some, cloth seats are fine. Then there is shape. The seats may be oversized or sculpted. They may feel cushy like a sofa or form-fitting like an Aeron chair. There is an examination of comfort. The shopper will have to adjust the seat right away, so those levers or controls are an immediate signal of the type of experience the manufacturer has created. A lever under the front edge of the seat is a manual tool. Electric controls signify something else. Are they a row of complicated controls or something simple to figure out without looking down?

Once the customer is in the seat, they take in the dash and console. They examine the displays. The styling of standard components like the fuel gauge and speedometer are critical points of comparison. There is a mental benchmark for each thing the shopper takes in and they are weighing it as they observe.

The customer's hands go to the steering wheel. Leather, plastic, composite. They feel the texture, and explore individual finger divots or hand rests. The wheel may be smooth, or grippy and the size of the wheel is quickly marked; it can be tilted up or down easily.

The controls on the wheel itself are quickly scanned. The driver wants to see how many features the car has compared to their previous cars and to others they are considering. People like progress. We typically do not like to go backwards. Once a person has had a feature, they are resistant to giving it up. This applies to features we love and sometimes features we never use. The steering wheel controls provide a quick inventory of those features.

Every part of a product and experience is an opportunity to communicate the specific brand. Each of these elements build a series of stories. The shoppers write the story as they go. And they either create the story around themselves or around somebody else. The stories are the facets of the brand. One facet may be entertaining the passengers, as in the SUV shopping mom we talked about earlier. Or there may be a facet about safety built around features. Customers do not consciously ask themselves whether they see themselves in a story, that only happens in focus groups. Instead, they receive signals and decide whether the facets are telling a story about them or about someone else.

Cars are interesting cases because of how many tactile and sensory features there are. The combination pulls in a customer or may repel them immediately. It is not common for someone to end up at a dealership of a brand they are not familiar with in a model they have never seen. Cars are also interesting because it remains a category that most people research thoroughly before they invest time in a visit. Sure they research performance and fuel economy, but they are also looking for signals that the vehicle is made for them.

Driving a car is one of the most honest brand experiences there is. The daily commute of your own car or starting up a rental puts you at one with the brand. You literally put your life into the brand. A shopper may spend hours on the website while looking for information and configuring features. They may find a car that has everything they think they want within their budget. But the screens may offer a clunky UX that makes them question the technology. Or buttons on the dash that make them wonder if the car is for someone older. Or a test drive with a salesperson they find annoying.

For a long time, almost all rental cars were base models. As a frequent traveler with no loyalty to a rental company, I would be randomly assigned a vehicle and never upgraded. I was introduced to many brands through rental companies in their base models. It never made sense to me. Here, I am in a new city, excited to get moving and in my first Hyundai ever. I was already driving when they launched here in the US and still had the perception that they were low cost, low quality cars. Until I drove one from Budget and thought they were even lower cost and lower quality. Why? Because there were no bells and whistles.

I thought then and still believe that auto manufacturers should only deploy upgraded models to rental fleets for this exact reason. You might never get a driver to your lot, but you can expose them to your brand serendipitously, and that chance should not be wasted. Each driver can be impressed by your product or depressed by it, but as a brand what is that impression worth to you? The materials, design, color ways, typefaces, technology, ergonomics are all up to the company and how they can be specific.

Burger King, Wendy's and McDonald's are the big three in quick service burger restaurants. Their menus and experience are all very similar. But so are their colors. They each use heavy servings of red with yellow, following a convention based on attracting motorists to their restaurant signage. It is hard for the runners-up to gain any ground on McDonald's in this paradigm because visual differentiation keeps them all in the same position. At this point, each of the three has equity in the red so changing is next to impossible. The next biggest challengers? Carl's Jr. / Hardee's, Jack in the Box, Checker's / Rally's and In-n-Out Burger all use a dominant red.

Some brands have appeared on the scene with a product built to challenge McDonald's. Brands like Five Guys and Smashburger sell hamburgers that are higher quality at a slightly higher price point. They are built on the traditional fast-food menu—hamburgers and French fries—but present the food in a way that feels more crafted and less mass-produced. They each opted to use red as their logo color to capitalize on the prevailing convention of red connecting to hamburger stands and missed an immediate opportunity to differentiate. True, the experience is very different from the QSR category, but it takes a visit to understand that. Thus a person comparing prices via Google Maps or Yelp! may never take a moment to compare the experience. They will align the brands by color and menu and triangulate price based on what they have been paying their entire life as a customer of McDonald's. *Why pay more? Is it worth it?* The specifics of flavor and experience are big for fast casual, but customers have to try it to get it.

How important are specifics to service brands? A new interaction mimics the feel of that first entry into the car. It yields an instantaneous reaction. How important is the lobby of a hotel to your belief in the brand? Not the finishes, but the shape, the layout, the music, the ambiance. And yet, so many miss. It is hard to forget a hotel you stayed at with a crappy elevator, and yet so many times you get into a gross elevator. Yes, the materials matter along with the staff and service itself. Hotels have this odd way of always promising personalized service and experience while avoiding tests of that service. I do have hotel loyalty, so I try to use the programs to improve my travel. Despite filling out a profile and staying many times, I have never received any perk or element of service that made me feel like they had done anything with all the data they have collected about me. This is not the kind of data I would feel creepy about. I volunteered it.

For example, I have simple taste when it comes to coffee. Always black. And never decaf. I do not use creamer or sugar. Anywhere I can give a preference on this front, I have. Still, every hotel room I've stayed in for the past 20 years has continued to provide me with many options for coffee that I would never drink (decaf) instead of an extra pod of regular, and always includes the creamer and sugar kit along with tea.

Every time I'm logging on to the hotel Wi-Fi and seeing their messaging reminder about their commitment to personalized attention, I laugh while sorting through all the decaf. *Yup, you guys totally get me.*

So much of user-centered design is thought of in terms of software product design, and with good reason. Once a customer sets a preference in software, it is set. Yet in terms of customer design, most retailers and service providers like hotels have extended no commitment to remembering those preferences. Thinking through specifics of customer experience design is going to be more critical as time goes on. Each innovation in software and technology raises our expectations as customers of all businesses going forward. Once there was a time when calling a cab was hassle. Now it's easy, one or two taps, no dispatcher or repeating addresses. When something once trying becomes simplified, it is natural to ask "Why is this other task not as simple as calling a Lyft?"

It is why Amazon Go is making cashierless grocery stores. They are looking for places to make improvements that people have not recognized that they need. The cashier is a product of the store not having a better way to capture payment and track inventory. It has never been part of satisfying customer needs. Specific design means planning the materials and the experience. In this case, it has given Amazon an instant benefit and point of distinction from every grocer on the planet. Amazon is optimizing its experience to reduce shopping friction. It is possible traditional retailers like

Safeway and Walmart could counter with more helpful, better trained staff to add a better personal experience.

Returning to our hamburger example, quick service restaurants all work the same way. There is usually a line leading to an order, and this might be standing or driving up. Neither feels too different from the other. These companies have each been flirting with apps and touchscreen kiosks, but it seems their specific consumers are more comfortable with the old way. Looking for a way to differentiate, Five Guys offers something no other brand in the category does. Upon entry, customers are used to finding the back of the line. In Five Guys restaurants, the back of the line is marked by a waist high box of peanuts and paper baskets. "Welcome," they beckon. Something small and different at the outset of the experience. A detail worth remembering, and potentially off-putting (especially if you've got a peanut allergy). But the brand puts a choice just inside the front door to reach their specific customer that will separate them from all their red competitors. It is a visual cue that the food is cooked in peanut oil, unique among large burger chains. Details like these are not what you would traditionally consider 'design' but are what create specific brands.

Specific : Adam Pierno

TELLING STORIES

There is no myth, story or anything produced by a brand that does not carry a message. Everything communicates the brand and signals who the brand exists to serve. Every company has its founding story. The two people in a garage working after-hours to build a product they knew the world needed.

Just because every company has one does not make them all equally interesting.

Since we are talking about story, we should start with words. Marketers tend to use the words 'company' and 'brand' interchangeably. But they are different words with different meanings. A company is a practical thing. It is a collection of people, processes, products. A company exists to achieve a business goal. A company has the goal of producing profit for designated stakeholders. Brands are something else. Brands are an idea. Brands are more like time, conceptually. Both are technically inventions, authored by someone, but inherently agreed upon by those that are exposed to it. Companies that become brands must become something more than practical to achieve this level of understanding. The actual story of a company's start is not usually inspiring.

The story—like the company—is full of practical details. A brand does not have to be practical. The founding story of a company can become the *myth* of the brand if the right enhancements find the right audience. When the people at the company understand the motivating insight of their specific customer, they begin to shape the story into a myth to lure that customer. They exclude some of the practical details. They embellish others. Some even make some up (some hire others to write it—gasp!). The story is crafted with the audience in mind. At this point, the founding transforms from a story (company) into a myth (brand). The details are passed from person to person in and out of the organization creating something greater than the truth, while not altogether untrue. It's not a fiction, but it is not exactly the truth, either.

Ultimately the truth is dull, and it is almost always this way when it comes to starting a business. People love to tell stories about their own children, but only a handful of those stories are interesting to others. So it goes with business stories as well. Only those who love the brand will have an interest in the story, and only the most interesting parts of the story will be worth telling anyone else. These are the parts that, in rare cases, become myth. A brand does not need to have a founding myth to be successful. It is one way some brands have developed. For many, many companies the facts of their founding and growth are simply too pedestrian to have the magic required to create a myth worth sharing.

Myths are powerful stories built on a belief system (the mythology). Myths only become powerful when they are valued enough to be passed from person to person. To be shared intimately; not broadcast. Traditionally, myths have been used to help explain things we have not been able to know or to understand. This definition would also cover the foundations of many religions—stories to explain science and nature that could not be understood. Author Robert Graves said in the introduction to *New Larousse Encyclopedia Of Mythology* that religion is only considered mythology by people who do not practice that religion. Those who practice the religion take the stories as truth. Granted, brands are not religion but the idea that concept rejectors will also reject myths about the brand apply here as well.

The Coca-Cola Company has crafted their brand myth about Doc Pemberton's discovery of the perfect recipe for the original beverage. More practical study of facts reveals a different side of the story and details that paint the man—and therefore the company—in a different light. The same is true of rival Pepsi. Caleb Bradham founded the drink in 1893 and the rest isn't exactly smooth sailing. The brand was founded in fits and starts for the first quarter century and those missteps are not included in the brand canon. The version of each story you are more inclined to believe, of the facts you are willing to include, is based on the brand you prefer. It is likely the story contributes to your preference for that brand in the first place.

When we are talking about myths, we should be discussing larger-than-life concepts. The reverence people have for Steve Jobs goes beyond the CEO of a technology company. His myth has converted him into a business Paul Bunyan and made Apple a legendary brand. Meanwhile, there have been hundreds of CEOs in Silicon Valley who have done amazing things, but none are described with the same reverence. It takes a myth to explain the cognitive power and discipline that created a company able to achieve all that Apple has. We mere mortals cannot fathom the undertaking. We use myth to help us understand.

PayPal was considered just a company—not a powerful consumer brand—by most. A successful company (practical), but not a great brand (myth). PayPal has never done any famous advertising. It has not made many memorable brand statements. It is a solid financial company, but not a specific brand. It was not important when the company was disrupting a traditional financial services space, because its service filled a need in a way competitors couldn't match. It is important today because it is now in the established role and challenger and established competitors have begun pecking away at its share. But PayPal was not always ready to be a specific brand.

This has changed over time as now-famous executive Elon Musk has gone on to bigger and crazier excesses. His myth (and those of other executives who have gone on to achieve greatness) carry the brand. Now that there is a mythical figure, the story of the original organization can be re-told and repackage PayPal as a brand. Along with the story of PayPal's original customers. Ebay users, looking for a way to conduct transactions digitally. Suddenly, Musk and his team are cast as pioneers (they were) though he only joined through a merger once PayPal had already tasted success. And the extremely practical business problem PayPal was solving is scripted into a vision of shaping the internet of the future.

Why does any of this matter? Because the current target customer for PayPal needs that story to understand the relevance of the brand today. The specific customer today needs to know how PayPal stands apart from and compares to new fintech, blockchain and brands like Venmo and Zelle. Of course there are practical differences between the companies and their business models, but not great enough differences to elevate PayPal above this new group of competitors. A myth sets the foundation of the company in a light that relates it to an audience that wasn't even alive when the brand was solving a very vexing problem and has many choices to address it today. It was a practical challenge then, but PayPal has begun telling and retelling it as myth.

Myths are only shared by people who have a relationship to them. People who believe those founding myths of their religion have a bond to the myth themselves. For example, you may have been told the myths of Christianity. In all likelihood, this was shared by a Christian. They connect to the details in a way that makes them share the story. The more they connect, the more passionately they share the myth along with the personal significance. Part of the teller's identity is wrapped up in this myth. *This myth has this meaning to me, so I am sharing it with you.* The myth is an attempt to make a connection between the person sharing and the recipient.

When people pass on a tale they don't connect with, it is told as a mere story; an urban legend. Urban legends are often shared as happening to a loose acquaintance, *a friend of a friend*. The looser connection to the story insulates the teller from ridicule and minimizes their investment. For PayPal, the story had been told by people one generation removed from passionate customers; people with no connection to the product and no tangible reason to take in details of the story. Without a belief in the myth, Paypal's story translated to "just like Venmo only more complicated." As a myth it translates to "a group of digital visionaries transformed the way currency was exchanged on the web."

For Apple, building its myth has become easier with each successful product launch. It was hard in the early 1990's when putty colored hard drives were commodities in the PC world. Steve Jobs became brilliant when the jewel colored iMac was released; a genius when the iPod launched, and a deity with he introduced the iPhone. Why? It is no coincidence, that the number of people who owned an Apple product increased over that time. Sales and the growth of Jobs' legend are linked. If we were all using Compaq computers and Motorola phones, the myth of Steve Jobs would still exist, but be limited to those customers of the 90's who loved the Apple operating system.

People have been trained to rank stories. We value myths at the top, then stories, then messages way down at the bottom. The story about a meeting at PayPal is considered less valuable than someone telling another about a meeting in which Steve Jobs dressed down an engineer. We are less invested in one than the other. When thinking specifically, the important piece is that the brand facets are transmitted to the person who will most value them.

We over-value the myth. Mythology is as old as man. But it is not a tool that can be stamped out by any company. Some companies just will not be myth-worthy. We once used myths to explain how the sun rises, or why we should appreciate the wisdom of our elders. Now we just want them to make our company seem worth buying from. If a brand myth is going to be effective, it must work on two levels. First, it has to be larger than life. It has to depict something nearly impossible, a revelation. How did that person face down that huge competitor? How did they think of this innovation? How could they have figured that out? It has to be a story worth telling. The founder needs to be inspired by a force outside themself. They need to overcome huge odds. They need to have a vision. And these things need to be bigger than the average person can imagine.

Second, the people who feel connected to it will be compelled to share it. Therefore, the brand needs to identify the audience's stake in the story. They need to have a grasp of the details as it pertains to their own experience. In the retelling it becomes their story. They become a part of the brand. The brand myth needs both the origin and the embellishment to be propagated.

Groupon is an example of a brand with many personal experiences, but no divine inspiration. Nothing amazing led to its founding. The original CEO was an accidental founder who was dismissed as the company faced stalling growth. Though millions of consumers used the service, few have details about the service itself that makes the origin myth more valuable or worthy of retelling. It is a fine corporate story, but there is nothing to build on.

The story of *Slender Man* did not grow because it was especially compelling. In fact, its vague origins demonstrate how important audience participation is. *Slender Man* is an urban legend. People should not be so passionate about sharing, because they have no stake in its propagation. Each of the original viewers who shared it added the sketchy details that made it something worth investigating further. The character peaked before it became a real movie. In fact, when it finally became a mass market film, it flopped because it was too defined and left the control of the community of authors and contributors who nurtured the original myth. Each person had expanded the myth in their retelling. They were invested. They made it their own. Once a screenwriter and director took it over, it was no longer the property of the community and they weren't interested in telling new people the story anymore.

The shape of story has changed dramatically since the Greeks began retelling their myths. And probably more, since the internet began decentralizing video distribution. Because most brand origins are dull, they need to engage their audience. How can a brand let their best customers take part in the myth? What part can the company give over to the customers? This was the promise of social media, letting customers 'join the conversation.' They never wanted to do that, but they will take experiences with the brand and make them part of the story they tell. Or they will re-share exceptional experiences (both positive and negative) that they hear happened to a friend of theirs. Or a friend of a friend. Sound familiar?

STORY

Suppose you were going to read a story to your young child at bedtime. They are four or five years old and snuggled in bed in their comfiest pajamas. You settle up, leaning back against the headboard. They yawn as you crack open the book. Chapter one, page one of *Pet Sematary.* What response do you expect from your child? Maybe this feels like a bad idea. Do you think the child will sleep soundly? Or ever?

Another example. You enter the church and find your seat. You greet the people around you. The pastor comes out and after a prayer begins a sermon. "My friends, I have a story to share with all of you. It was crazy, we went to Vegas and I have never been so wasted." Stop right there. This group doesn't want to hear it. This is not a story we want from our pastor. Or any pastor.

Based on these examples, it is clear that knowing our audience makes for successful stories. This is another reason to know the customer the brand is being created for. The story of the company, of its founding is no different. It is usually crafted and shaped to appeal to the end user.

Facebook's story has remained largely unchanged since Mark Zuckerberg began marketing to schools beyond Harvard. Curious and driven, he was interested in creating a way for students to connect, build relationships and grow together. But over the decade and a half since then, different parts of the story have been the focus. As a brash entrepreneur, the focus was on his drive; Zuckerberg famously shared business cards reading 'I'm CEO, bitch.'

Classy.

As the company and his family grew, he began to focus on his legacy. The story had a new focus. It shifted to his desire to *connect the world* as he spoke of his family foundation and charitable giving. This became a refrain when he was dragged in front of congress after the 2016 elections.

Believers in the company (and shareholders, probably) lean towards the positive attributes of the story. They help shape it by telling the details that they can support. In David Fincher's film, *The Social Network*, the story keys in on several more salacious points like the Winklevoss twins and the early involvement of Sean Parker. Critics of the company are more likely to latch onto these.

The same is true of McDonald's founding story and the man who gets the credit for making the brand, Ray Kroc. People who love the brand hold him up as a model of dedication and efficiency. The film, *The Founder* delves into the man's ambition and challenges his integrity in his dealings with the McDonald brothers, who opened the original hamburger stand that inspired him. Critics of fast food are more likely to tell these negative aspects. The story is shaped by both the storyteller and the receiver.

Every story has an author and every author has an audience for each story. Ray Kroc's biographer has a story for fans of the McDonald's brands and what it stands for. McDonald's detractors have another story for those opposed to things like globalized food production. The way the author connects to that audience makes the story a medium for connection between the two. Many companies wait for that story to be written, but brands figure out their specific audience, and write the story for them, leaving space for the audience to add new ideas. Brands earn the privilege of customers and fans adding their personal experience as they retell the story.

This is not the first time you have read about storytelling being an important part of branding, to be sure. Specific brands have a different approach to their story. The best stories are not those that are just enjoyed during the telling. True, that is certainly a part. We read, watch or listen to be entertained, and we will not finish the story if it is not interesting and engaging in some way. But how many times have you stopped a movie on Netflix halfway through just because it was not holding your attention? Or stopped mid-workout to skip a podcast episode. Or that book you just never pick up again.

The first rule of telling a brand story is to make it a good story. A story worth hearing. Unskippable. But, the story is what it is, right? Not exactly. Journalists and documentarians take true stories and craft them into compelling narratives that lock our attention. *Making a Murderer* is a Netflix series that many people could not stop watching because it was so interesting and kept throwing twists and turns. The story is the telling of an investigation of a missing person and the small town politics and relationships behind it. It *is* a documentary, but the story has a point of view. The filmmakers edited the story to time out twists and turns for dramatic effect, creating drama.

Making a Murderer was constructed to take a story that had been effectively summarized in the news blotter and bring it to life. The story hinges on making details of the investigation look like they have blamed the wrong person. With each episode, the story expands to reveal more of the local relationships and back story that lead to alleged bias against the accused. The show turned the bullet points of the crime into a dramatic nail biter, a story worth watching.

Mr. Robot is a fine TV show (remember those?) airing on USA. As a standalone story, it has earned awards since its first season. For people more interested in the story, the show's producers have added breadcrumbs in and around each episode that can be searched online to add context to the world depicted in the series. The show is about a hacker who brings down a fictional tech giant (Ecorp) along with the end of the global economy.

Each episode features multiple websites, apps, intranets and coding terminals with IP addresses. As watchers quickly learned, *Mr. Robot's* producers own every website and IP address shown on screen, and then some. Reddit users began tracking the websites and connecting the dots between on-screen dialogue, locations in the show, and making connections that add richness to the story and joy to the viewers. The clues range from simple to find (a well executed faux-customer email sent by Ecorp) to the complex (hosting users at a terminal they may attempt to hack using code from an episode). These Easter eggs make the story worth sharing. Instead of saying to a friend, "This is a good

TV show," the myth is made up of something more. "This TV show also happens online, I was able to hack into a website from the show using dialogue as a clue!"

A good story is table stakes. There must be something more to make it myth. The next rule is to make the story worth telling someone else about, and making your specific customer a character in the tale. Disney is a fantastic examples of this. The Disney brand is a sprawling empire that covers princesses, cartoons, superheroes and a galaxy far, far away. They produce many of the remaining shared experiences in pop-culture. These are huge events. Through the collection of games and amusement park experiences, Disney makes these larger-than-life things personal. When a parent sees their child run toward Mickey Mouse or hug Princess Anna at the Magic Kingdom, they tell that immediately gain a story to share. When gamers use a character in *Kingdom Hearts*, they have a connection and a first-person experience as Buzz Lightyear or Beast that they can talk about with their friends. Disney is great at producing stories at scale, and perhaps even more clever about getting their audience to create their own.

THE WHY AND PURPOSE

Here is what people want to know. Why did the company's founders go through the trouble of starting the brand?

Why do you do the things you do every day? Are those things a part of the story that is interesting to your specific customer? Are those things going to get those people talking about your business?

There is a big focus on corporate purpose today. What is the brand doing to improve the world? Every brand is looking for a hook to make their story go and purpose can be a powerful one. But a lot of companies have resorted to duct taping a purpose on to an existing business model and writing a press release about it.

There are many, many great organizations that exist to solve problems in the world. Some of these are charitable organizations, others are commercial entities that are built to raise money for a cause as their primary mission. There are also companies with a mission built in. Tom's Shoes and Warby Parker have the 'we give one to people with a need' for shoes and eyeglasses as part of their business model. Those companies have built a following based on their mission, the perceived quality of their products as well as their aesthetic. The purpose is part, but not all. Purpose is one facet of those brands.

When a company has a cause baked in at inception that makes sense for both the company and for the customer it is a tremendous part of their story. The myth connecting these pieces together will carry far, especially when it meets the customer at their motivating insight. And if that purpose is bringing sight to everyone in the world, even better. It is clear, it is useful and it is hard for the customer to object to.

It is not mandatory that every company cure a social, health or environmental problem in the world. Again, nobody cares about your product or service. Or more precisely, they care about it for exact amount of time they are interacting with or using it. Then they probably don't care again until they need it next. Brands don't need to apologize for being commercial enterprises that solve their specific problem well, but do not save the world. The purpose trend is tied to the new shortage of attention for brands. Brands are trying to expand the ways they can be thought of beyond the product that is easy for consumers to put out of mind. But it is more than OK for the company to have the sole purpose of producing the solution to a specific problem only, with no expanded social purpose.

Whatever the purpose, it needs to be articulated. Clearly. Giant companies have broad purposes. At the global level, the why is, "We will provide branded products and services of superior quality and value that improve the lives of the world's consumers, now and for generations to come. As a result, consumers will reward us with leadership sales, profit and value creation, allowing our people, our shareholders and the communities in which we live and work to prosper." Sure.

Procter & Gamble has not traditionally sold directly to consumers. The above purpose is written for shareholders. It is meant to convince them the company will return value. It is a specific purpose for that specific buyer. The bigger the company the more bland the purpose. Safe and toothless. Its specific purpose is to not frighten buyers of the stock away. This company is not a risk with your money.

As it relates to consumers, P&G breaks its product purpose into individual reasons why, in order to make any sense at all to customers. Tide, Gain, Bounty, Iams and Ariel (and dozens of others) will each have to have a tighter purpose that is relevant and meaningful to each core group of customers. That long-winded gobbledygook would not reach anyone at the grocery level. Tide's stated brand purpose is to renew clothes and the story clothes tell. People can figure out why that purpose belongs in their basket for themselves. Why? Because of the great brand story of Tide? Think about it for a moment. What is Tide's story?

Tide is a mega brand that achieved dominance during the golden age of mass media, CPG advertising. Tide has no story and certainly no myth. It is now at a dominant scale that is virtually impossible to undo. It would take dozens of challengers with tremendous myths, along with several "kids eating Tide Pod" sized catastrophes, to unseat Tide. For a brand to compete with Tide, it will need a story that quickly becomes myth.

When a product is created in a boardroom, for the sole purpose of filling a market need, people know it. They are looking for that story that speaks to them specifically. Greek yogurt is a multi-billion dollar category in the US. The category leader, Chobani, is the only one with such a story. Founded in upstate New York by a Turkish immigrant. The brand name translates to 'shepherd,' and shepherd it did. Not only did it change the palate for yogurt in America, but the brand's founder is a leader in employment and leadership.

He sets his own minimum salaries for staff that vastly out-pace the US minimum wage, and hires a mix of locals and refugees. They set the standard for the product and category, and added a purpose that is creating a myth relevant to its core consumers. But why?

People want to know a company cares about making a product that solves the problem they have. And the myth helps get that across to specific customers. Whether it is through the founder deity or the purpose they went to work to address. It needs to be crystal clear what you want the brand to do and the reason why.

While the flavor of Greek yogurt is very specific as an attribute, it fails as a purpose. It fails as a myth for sure. And yet, the product sells. Is the myth required? No, certainly not. A story is required, but not in the sense that we traditionally think of 'stories.' But Hamdi Ulukaya taking a stand on labor and immigration issues is helping to build the myth alongside product they love.

Author, Kurt Vonnegut had a presentation he would share on the *shape* of story. In the presentation, he charts stories on two axes: First, good fortune and ill fortune. Next, a timeline, beginning to end. The story starts with a protagonist doing moderately well, above halfway to good fortune. As we move to the middle of the story, there's an inciting incident that moves their fortune deep into ill territory. Finally, the protagonist takes action, or the gods smile on her, and the story resolves, with the main character back in good fortune.

Usually slightly better off than they were at the start. "We love this story!" he says, pointing at the graph.

That is how we have all been taught to think about stories. Beginning, middle, end. Drama, action, resolution! There is nothing dramatic about yogurt. But Chobani customers are transmitting this story from person to person to help build its sales, brand and myth. Chobani grew to $1.5 billion in sales despite having no myth, on the merits of its product alone. Now, as the stories of founder, Hamdi Ulukaya spread, people are getting a sense of the purpose. The brand is getting the reaction they desire. They are getting one person to tell the next.

The Steve Jobs myth is a fantastic way to transmit Apple's facet of innovation. He was relentless when developing products. On the surface level these stories speak to his drive and focus. But like many myths it explains the reputation their products have for surpassing user expectation. Chobani has no myth that communicates the benefit. The benefit is communicated by word-of-mouth by people who experience it and appreciate it. A cup of yogurt sells for around a dollar. The brand does not need a myth at this price level. If the brand has greater ambitions to expand beyond its core category, the myth it is been building will help get it there.

In some cases exclusivity and myth are interchangeable. Maseratis are expensive. Most consumers don't know why. Each time the average driver sees a Maserati, they are reminded only about how rare they are. There are not many well-known stories that average consumers can recall about the Maserati brand or vehicles. They would be hard pressed to name a Maserati model. The exclusivity is the myth that justifies the price and exclusivity. With each encounter, the value ratchets up another level. We expect a Maserati to be expensive and we are reassured that it is.

Remember, almost nobody cares about your product or brand. It is a transaction. They think about the barbecue sauce just when they are shaking it onto their plate, and then not until the next time they need it. OK, they might think about it a bit more than a Maserati. Not every company has a meaningful mythology, but every great brand does. This is what separates specific from transaction. When it comes to common purchases, we want people to have mental maps of the seventeen ingredients in our sauce and connect those to a concert sponsorship series that was executed in 2005. They do not. They do not read the website. They do not share the Instagram posts. They do not want the myth. It is more likely to be created externally or accidentally. It is more likely that the brand myth is incidental to some other story than to be the creation of the brand team or agency. That does not mean to ignore the potential of myths or stories. A brand with a powerful myth provides the mental availability needed for the consumer to remember the product. That what being specific means.

Specific : Adam Pierno

WITH INTEREST

You are asking at this point, "How can anyone build a brand if nobody is interested in my company?"

I assure you, I am not being figurative when I say that nobody is interested in your company.

We misunderstand what interest in companies is or can be. Here is what people are interested in, their job, family, friends, commute, food, sex life, health, pets, education, entertainment, hobbies. There may be one or two that I forgot. They think about products for the time that they need the solution, or are thinking about improving or addressing any of those interests listed above.

Marketers tend to spend a lot of time imagining all the ways people are actively or passively thinking about their products. We map out the customer journey, as if the customer agrees that they are on one. They have no idea. They see cool shoes, they Google "shoes." It is 11:40, they think about lunch. They are not following a matrix of Post-it notes and dry erase marker doodles along a pathway to investigate any of these things.

As discussed earlier, people do care inordinately about hobbies, entertainment and sports. They are passionate about their sports teams, because those teams and players become an extension of themselves.

It was once location based, and the team was a representation of where the fans lived or were from. But now, rooting for a team says something more personal. I can root for Juventus, Tokyo Giants, New York Jets and Dynamo Kiev from my home in Phoenix. That collection of teams says something about who I am. I have chosen those teams, they align with who I am. They help define who I am.

The games those teams play are fun to watch on TV or streaming. But there are so many more ways to engage with the teams than games alone. Every league has its own channel, so fans can watch other league games or classic games. There is also news and content. There are jerseys, kits, apparel and merchandise to shop for. There are player social media accounts. There are 30-for-30s on ESPN. A fan can spend time with any of or all of these things. They can share these with fellow fans or rival fans. This does not even account for fantasy sports.

This is what interest looks like. People are passionate about the things that capture their attention and imagination. Passion like this is also true for movies, music, gaming and pop culture. As we have discussed, those things are created for a specific audience to elicit a specific reaction. But brands? No. Even the consumer brands with the most engaging mythology do not generate this level of interest. Nobody gets this excited about national pizza chains, paper towels, blow dryers or board games. Nobody invests a fraction of the energy that they invest in their passions, in products like these. We don't want to engage emotionally with products at all, but when we take an interest a brand can earn emotional credit.

When the door cracks open during that tiny timeframe in which they have the need, the opportunity arises for people to become interested in a product temporarily. Just at the moment when they recognize they will need to decorate for Christmas, they are—for a few minutes—interested in a way to hang a wreath on the door. They may go to straight to Amazon, they may go to YouTube or Google. Maybe Pinterest. Probably not more than two of those sites. Perhaps they want to actually touch a hook so they go to Michael's craft stores. They buy one, it works. They never think about it again. The door is closed on interest.

Smuckers recently announced a new approach to branding. This company has been around for as long as I have (longer, in fact). In a statement about their new brand efforts, of course a representative referenced brand love. But he spent more time talking about scale, innovation and distribution. Let's get specific.

People do not think about Smuckers. Ever. Not never, but almost never. When they do think about Smuckers they are thinking about jelly. Smuckers sells peanut butter, ice cream topping and Uncrustables frozen sandwiches, but people think of jelly first, second and third. How often do you think about jelly? If you do think about it, a word cloud would reveal that there are about five keywords that make up those thoughts. In descending order: buy, almost out, flavor, peanut butter, bread. Jelly is essentially a more frequent wreath hanger.

That is an oversimplification of course. Since jelly is food often consumed by children of the shopper, it is a higher consideration purchase. But it is not a car. It is not your favorite football team. Distribution and scale are much more important than myth here. If a customer remembers they need to buy more jelly, the jelly better be there when they stop to buy it. Innovation? 80-90% of declared innovation is for the benefit of the board room and investors. Most people that buy jelly are OK with the current formats and are not clamoring for new ways to consume it. They really are not thinking about it much at all, besides making lunch and buying the products needed to make lunch. It's not all that interesting. Perhaps the most interesting thing the brand can do then, the way to make their specific customer love the brand is to be as widely available as possible, and be available in the format they want and expect.

Let's say Smuckers goes all in on innovation. They come up with three new products in the next year. Three non-jelly products, in an effort to expand their portfolio, and enter the outer aisle where grocery traffic has largely moved. They move their production and distribution focus to these new products. Current buyers continue to need jelly. They go to the center of the store once a week to buy Smuckers jelly. But one day, it isn't there. At the time they allotted to get to the grocery store. The only time. They buy something else. They may try one more time to buy Smuckers a week or two later. If they can't easily find it, they might be customers of the replacement brand forever. The habit is changed.

They're not interested in Smuckers. They do not love it. They are interested in their family and achieving the task of making lunch. That's it. They appreciate that Smuckers is a product that helps them do that. But if the price goes up dramatically, or the flavor changes, or if it moves in the store, it will be replaced.

It is not the Pittsburgh Steelers. It's just jelly. It is not that interesting. Except for the specific three-and-a-half minutes that it is. Everything is a transaction based on immediate needs. So much of what we do is dedicated to trying to create that interest in our customer. We want them to become interested through content, or shopping. But we bore them with "content" about the product, or try to disguise the content as something that is not an ad. This is nuts. We need to understand and admit that our customers might just not care about our product. We should not try to compete with the Toronto Maple Leafs or Cardi B. or Netflix. Instead we should maximize the tiny crack in the door to make our product as easy to understand and buy in that time and space.

A woman plugs in her flat iron and finds that it is dead, and the door cracks open. She suddenly has interest. But what she wants to know depends on a few factors.

If she liked the flat iron she's been using, she may just be interested in finding the same exact product to replace it. She will go to the manufacturer's website and try to find the product number. If it's there she may order it, or she may then look to see if there has been an improvement or upgrade, and then shop based on features and cost.

If she has a trip coming, she may only care about replacing it as soon as she can. Go to Amazon, look for shipping options. What can be delivered before the trip?

She may have been getting bored of her hair and thinking of changing the style. She might then look for a new product that can add a different style like a curl or a wave. In this case she may seek reviews of new products or go to fashion magazines for tips.

These are three of hundreds of potential responses to the dead flat iron. Because it is difficult to predict what a person's interest will be, every eventuality needs to be addressed. This is how we misunderstand interest. We assume that people will be interested and go on some journey collecting the bread crumbs we leave from beginning to end - taking in every detail. Interest is customers accidentally finding their own door into our maze and looking for their own way to the point they determine to be the finish.

Take the logic out of it. This woman came to believe this flat iron made her beautiful. It gave her confidence. This emotion didn't come from an ad or content. It came from using the product and learning to trust it. Replacing it doesn't suddenly make her interested in 'learning more' about flat irons, or 'joining the conversation' on their social channels. It creates an urgency to get her confidence back.

As a marketer, today's puzzle is figuring out how to prepare for interest in whatever form it arrives, on demand. That does not diminish the responsibility of building awareness. Everything we do for brands cannot be conversion based. There are three distinct but related phases: awareness, interest and experience.

Travel provides an excellent way to understand this. The need for a trip arises. A person needs to travel from Oregon to Texas for an event. He considers options. He could drive, or take a bus. The train seems complicated. After thinking it over, he decides the easiest way is to fly. He is not a regular traveler, and he has to think about how to proceed. He goes to Google. He is unsure about the resulting shopping window on Google after putting the term "Flight Portland Houston" into the search bar. He scrolls down until he sees a sponsored result from Kayak. In fact, the entire first page of results is made up of sponsored and organic results for flight booking aggregators like Expedia, CheapoAir, Travelocity and Sky Scanner. There are no airlines listed. He remembers a Kayak ad he saw during *MasterChef*.

Clicking in, he thinks the prices seem higher than they should. He scans the results looking for ways to make it cheaper, or in some way better, than the results Kayak has produced. He thinks about past flights he has taken, and realizes there aren't results for Southwest and Delta. He now goes to search both sites individually, for those fares and expects Southwest to be cheapest. He's surprised to see that Kayak had cheaper rates and now, understanding the market clicks back to look at options again.

Having a new sense of pricing, he now turns focus to flight times. Based on his schedule, he chooses a flight on Alaska Airline. He has seen tons of outdoor and television ads for Alaska and feels comfortable with his choice knowing he is paying more than he expected, but flying with an airline he knows has convenient flight times.
That's it. He has no affinity. The journey isn't constructed

around Alaska's presence on Instagram or its recent YouTube influencer campaign. He booked on vectors that made his trip work better for him and didn't feel like he was getting a bad deal. Awareness isn't a direct trip to Alaskaair.com. Awareness helped capture interest during the short time it was there. Thanks to exposure effect, when the customer had a goal that required the brand, awareness helped get it considered.

So much is invested in conversion. Then comes the experience. Remember, he's chosen Alaska Airlines after searching on an online travel agent site. But he is a customer just the same. But the experience goes beyond the few things in the control of the airline. There is parking, transport, security, airport staff, restaurant and concession, bathrooms, all potentially before he even gets on the flight. All of those help shape his experience and impression of Alaska Airlines.

Interest helps us seek a solution. Understanding is how we make the choice. In the above example, our traveler has a need to travel. Upon investigating a set of options, he gains interest in several. Imagine if, instead of air travel, it was a brand category he had no exposure to at all. No awareness of any brand. He would still have a need, but would not be able to identify or separate one option from another.

Understanding of features, benefits—yes specifics about a brand that make it the right choice in a given situation. Imagine he was asked to buy an air hammer despite having no education about the product or usage. What vectors would he be using to decide which is best? He would have to do research at a category level, then a brand level, and *finally* a product level (assuming, of course he is a conscientious shopper. Just go with me here).

Interest would get him to category knowledge. He needs this tool to cut sheet metal. Understanding would tell him that the Chicago Pneumatic T012735 CP714 offers the best mix of flexibility and power, with an ergonomic handle and trigger that offers safety and control. Just the details he was hoping for, as he learned about the category. Understanding tells a consumer when to choose one product over another. He applied this same logic to choosing an airline for his trip. A brand he could count on with the detailed cost and schedule that satisfied his need.

Restaurant brands have a challenge in this area as well. Winning a dining occasion is hard. Competition is everywhere. National brands spend tons for awareness to capitalize when interest arises. When a meal occasion occurs, the brand is dependent on proximity, price, cuisine, loyalty and the estimated time of experience. The order of those factors changes, the more people involved in the meal and their relationships adds complexity.

Assume a group of people successfully navigates the selection process to choose a brand like Chili's. Awareness, interest and understanding have conspired here to drive selection. The group works through all the logistics to get there, and the experience now relies on the staff. What if it is dinner during the peak time on the busiest night of the week for that location?

A server called in sick. The host is stuck at a table and nowhere to be found, service is slow, the kitchen is way behind.

These people don't have a fantastic experience. Now the awareness of the brand becomes a challenge because this group has an interest in the brand, but it's not a positive one. Their favorability is down and they will associate the brand with the negative until something replaces it in their mind. Every time they are reminded of the brand, they will bring up the bad experience. That might mean a positive interaction with the brand or a worse (or more recent) negative experience with a different brand. This provides a new story for the customer to tell.

Consumer packaged goods brands need to think about all the ways grocery or retailers shape the experience around their brands as well. It is not easy to capitalize on a customer's interest, and traditional CPG brands are at the mercy of grocery staff. But if the shelves aren't stocked, or the product's been moved, if store personnel can't answer questions, it can reflect on the brand.

Interest is fleeting. A bad night for a server or a mess in the stock room and interest in your brand can be replaced. So much of the process is out of the control of the brand. Capitalizing on interest opportunities is critical. Awareness is not part of a determined funnel, but without awareness, a brand can not be considered.

ADVERTISING

As an insider, I am naturally skeptical (or maybe cynical?) about the effectiveness of advertising. I have difficulty putting faith in it, because I am exposed to advertising ideas in raw form for 8-16 hours per day and blot out as many inputs as possible after hours. Are ordinary consumers different? That is hard to objectively say.

In a study I conducted, we found that consumers identified with ads and recognized advertising's effectiveness. Of a national sample, spanning census representation for age, income, gender and political affiliation, more than half of respondents agreed that advertising influences their purchase decisions while only 21% disagreed.

We were probing to see if respondents were able to process the influences and how they perceived various advertising stimuli. They were also asked to name the separate qualities of commercials that they found most memorable and most persuasive. Two-thirds said funny commercials are the most memorable, and a majority of respondents (41%) said that 'informative' commercials are the most persuasive. When asking people to explain how they think, always take the results with a grain of thought. The point is not that funny ads work the best.

People notice different ad formats and categorize them as achieving different things. Our expectations of brand communications shifts as we recognize what type of message the brand is sharing, or what they are asking of us. We are in a passive conversation with the ad, recognizing for example, that the ad wants us to give them something back (such as a website visit) or just be entertained (and retain the brand message).

Consumers have expectations of categories as well. For example, they noted that car/truck and restaurant advertisers were more likely to be negative about a competitor. These expectations tell us that they are grouping together inputs. They can put all car ads into a descriptive set. They can put an entire platform like Instagram into a descriptive set of its own. Posts on Instagram look like *this*.

This is your decision point. Interest is difficult to earn. It is based on a combination of awareness, understanding and need. Category conventions are just that, conventional. Car ads show cars on wet, empty roads, often at night or driving across desert vistas. Restaurant ads always show someone take a bite and smile. Insurance ads are funny for some reason (thanks Geico). Intuitively, a person outside the category would say "If I got the chance to work on Mazda, it would be totally different. It needs to stand out." But as soon as they are brought in, they are pummeled into submission and begin to conform to the wicked conventions that keep the brands at similar levels of awareness, understanding and therefore - interest.

How can Mazda grow in differentiated understanding from other car makers when the difference between their ads remains a constant? The brand can take some calculated risks, like Kia did. Kia, in hopes of creating difference between itself and other cars at their price point introduced the hamsters. The hamsters were a gimmick that still allowed the brand to show off the car, but use a character in place of models to give the car and its drivers a visual difference from the pack. In their introductory spot, Kia featured footage of hamsters running in wheels, seemingly content to not move forward. Hard cut to a hip hamster in streetwear driving a Kia. One year later, sales were up 45% over the previous year. Kia wisely ran with the campaign until it ran out of steam a few years later, when consumers tired of the novelty of driving hamsters.

Toyota's Scion had tried a similar tact of presenting buyers of other cars as 'sheeple' in an earlier campaign that fell flat. The car and campaign was aimed at the same consumer, Gen Y buyers looking for style on a budget. Scion's spots were animated and dark. They identified their customers as 'deviants.' There were decapitations. It is pretty nuts. The hamsters delivered because the agency behind it figured out which convention to keep. They still managed to show the car on wet city streets. Everyone maintained possession of their head.

Maybe Scion had the right idea. A really specific vision that would appeal to their customer. It was different and it was bold. The Scion insight is the same as in the Kia campaign: Our drivers are not followers. In this case Scion was either too specific or had just chosen the wrong characteristics to express. The brand overestimated the ability of adjacent audiences to accept the idea. Deviance does not travel. By definition, deviance should not become a mass market idea. Scion drivers were depicted as snarling demons in the ads.

Scion was not able to expand outside their core audience and the brand was ultimately shrunk and folded back into the Toyota umbrella. Kia met their core customer where they were. The brand was able to recruit more lookalikes and others on the shoulders of the specific audience to their brand, by presenting a vision that was equal parts specific and attractive.

Chili's launched a short-lived campaign in which they depicted a fake restaurant competitor called PJ Blands. The idea? Chili's delivers flavor other casual dining chains don't. The execution? Confusing. The ads were pulled from the air and have even been scrubbed from the internet. It was certainly different, but it did something bad which both Kia and Scion avoided. It was negative about competitors.

Yes, both the car companies depicted a world in which their car was an antidote, but not another car. Not a competitor. Saying something negative about a competitor or the category is not necessarily the same as being specific and positive about your own brand. And people do not like the negative. In the same study referenced above, almost half of all respondents said negative ads make them feel badly about the advertiser, not the victim of the insults. Another 25% said negative ads make them curious about the brand being slammed.

Chili's didn't mention an actual brand by name, but the effect was the same. The ads were off the air within weeks and sales hit the floor. They did not differentiate themselves in a meaningful way to their customer. They smack talked the competitor, or maybe the entire category. This fails with consumers for a simple reason. People have category interest and are limited to the options they have. Sometimes they find themselves in those cardboard restaurants and they might be reading into the brand being represented by PJ Blands. When you judge that brand, you judge the consumers of that brand. It is rare for a person to have a binary relationship with options within a category. People who eat at Chili's are also probably receptive to concepts like Friday's, Outback and O'Charley's. Telling people why a competitor is bad is telling them 'you sometimes have bad taste.' And nobody wants to believe that about themselves.

Advertising has to capitalize on interest when it arises, and build understanding so when there is need, the consumer can act in the way the brand has suggested. In the US, there is television advertising for several whiskey brands. Jack Daniels, Gentleman Jack, Johnnie Walker, Wild Turkey, Jameson, Maker's Mark and Tincup are just some. Whiskey is not as frequently consumed as beer, and there is real preference by regular drinkers of one brand over others. There are distinctions in varietals. For example, I have included bourbon and Irish but excluded scotch brands, several of which are also advertising on television. When it comes to whiskey and bourbon, the ads never seem to stop. They are pure branding, some better executed than others. None of these campaigns include a call to action. The partial list above demonstrates the density of the competition for interest. Each brand is reaching out to a specific customer to build brand preference where there is overlap.

Most brands focus on the myth of the brand as Johnnie Walker did. Jack Daniels focuses on the brand story, reminding viewers about the small town in which it and its company values come from. Tincup has begun branding itself as the 'mountain whisky,' showing people enjoying it at a campfire after a long hike. Not sure if that improved preference for the brand, but probably increased US appetites for hiking. The outdoor setting is an example of ways brands are desperately seeking blue ocean to separate from the rest of the category as a means of increasing interest.

Jim Beam spent several years building its brand with a focus on its aging process. Using actress Mila Kunis as a spokesperson, the brand launched a spot showing her closing a barrel and literally branding it with her name. She commits to coming back for the barrel in "Four long years." Four years later (but they were just regular years, not any longer than other years. I checked), the campaign continued. A new spot showed Kunis returning to the barrel for a glass. This serialized ad is Jim Beam's long-term investment in brand understanding and sales have continue to grow. They have used an unexpected celebrity spokesperson to educate consumers in their distillation and aging process.

Recently, the Jim Beam campaign shifted to in-bar messages with a focus on ordering Jim Beam. Almost acknowledging the crowded category with a spot that shows a wall of bottles and suggests it may be too intimidating or confusing to choose. A couple standing at the bar decides to order Jim Beam (surprise!). The spot is consistent with the four-year-old campaign in tone and style. But the message is different. It is suggesting a need state, and potentially a consumer benefit. For newcomers to the category, the brand is both easy to remember and acceptable to order at an upscale function. Jim Beam already has high awareness in the US. They have leveraged Mila Kunis to maintain interest. Now they have increased understanding to pay off when there is a need. Sales in 2018 were up almost ten percent.

When you invest in awareness, you can control interest (Mila Kunis helps) and become the education source to drive category understanding and need. Each brand in the category is trying to win a specific segment of whiskey drinkers by engaging them with different interests to build an emotional connection. Jim Beam, craft. Tin Cup, bonding through nature. Maker's Mark, tradition.

The advertising, like the spirit attempts to connect on something more than alcohol content. Preference is driven by taste, yes, but also by perceived expressive benefit and memories and experiences people have while enjoying it. Wild nights or great conversations. People may grant interest temporarily. They give emotion involuntarily, succumbing when a product or service meets their needs in a special way.

Specific : Adam Pierno

PRICE AND VALUE

Earlier, we discussed Maserati as an example of a brand that is considered valuable, in part, because it is expensive. The price somehow seems to justify itself. Meanwhile, I just used Kia as an example of a brand effectively differentiating from the competitive set with advertising to increase sales of its more modestly priced cars. Both are true.

Price is not relative, but value is. When we're thinking about the design of the product from the perspective of our specific customer, we're thinking about all the elements that lead to its cost. And to its value. So that first feel of the driver's seat in the dealership goes a long way to meeting or exceeding the expectations of a buyer. Of course, a Maserati is not a Kia. They are made of different materials, in different ways, to meet a different design spec.

For some customers, a lower price will not compute. The person who can afford a top tier vehicle would probably not look at the entry-level vehicle in the manufacturer's lineup. The high price substantiates its value, and their own. For the Kia shopper, they are probably looking for a value in terms of an exchange of features for cost. Price and value are a complex trade off.

One of the key items in that trade off is awareness. Think about whiskey again. The brands most frequently on television are 'safe' brands. You can find them at any liquor store or even grocery stores where retail alcohol sales are legal. Awareness and distribution rule the day.

On a given Friday, picking up a bottle of Jack Daniels or Johnnie Walker is perfectly acceptable on your way to a friend's card game. $36. Worth it. These brands have crafted their story to be perfect for these purchases; easy, friendly, popular.

What about when the occasion is a little more special? Is a bottle of Jack still good enough? The occasion drives the value exchange up. Your kid brother passes the bar exam. 20th college reunion with the old roommates. A friend returns home from military service. You might want to buy something a little more... special. Special. You finished the sentence before you read it. The TV brands aren't special.

They are average. And why? They are made average by their mental and physical availability. They are available at drug stores. A great thing for sales, and for average Friday nights. But terrible for building an exclusive brand that commands higher price that *successfully feels like a value.* That's why people are willing to pay ridiculous sums for Pappy Van Winkle, on the rare occasion they can find a bottle for sale.

Neither the Kia nor the Maserati feels expensive to their specific buyers. No, it feels *worth it.* Why?

In a study I conducted on the buying habits of floor cleaning liquids, respondents were clear on this. The products tested ranged from 'home remedies' like vinegar and water to about a dozen commonly available household cleaning products. Each of these products had been established in the US for at least a decade, and had a chance to imprint specific audiences. Pricing was clustered from about $3 to $8 for a similar sized bottle.

Respondents who selected the highest priced product told us they felt is was a value at its $8 price point. But they also indicated they would still choose the product out of the same competitive set at over $10 and feel good about it. Why would they be willing to pay 25% more for the product? Because the brand made them feel reassured. In comparison to the lower-end brands, which made them feel anxious and unconfident about their cleaning duties, this brand made them feel assured and relaxed.

The customers buying the more expensive brand believed it not only solved the literal problem of cleaning the floor. But it also addressed the unspoken problem. The more expensive brand gave them confidence that they were taking care of their floor, had a lower chanced to damage it. It put them at ease. This product makes them feel they were making a better choice. They have an emotion response to the brand. The higher price is therefore justified.

The expensive cleaning product meets the core need: it gets the floor clean. But it has extra attributes that build on one another for this specific customer. It dries quickly, so there are no footprints or hovering while it dries. It is non-toxic, so it won't hurt kids or pets. Of course there are product benefits but there is also the brand. The brand is about making floors beautiful, not merely cleaning them. In advertising, they opt for moments of people living on their beautiful floors in lieu of demonstrations of cleaning them. Apparently, this resonates. It makes the extra cost acceptable.

Swiffer is the biggest brand in this category. But it did not fare well in price elasticity studies, meaning people said they would not pay more than its current retail price. The brand is about quick execution of a task, not about an end state.

Swiffer leads the conversation and has chosen to focus it on the task. It has been a successful strategy in terms of gaining market share and unit sales. Customers have been trained to price the task that Swiffer accomplishes, not the end state (i.e.. beautiful floors). Swiffer has been so effective at communicating the quickness of the task, and avoided conversation about deep cleaning that their specific customer has pegged a value on the brand. Procter & Gamble will have to launch a premium brand to make a major move up in cost per unit, a victim of their own success with Swiffer. There is an emotion involved in every purpose that is balanced against what goal the buyer has, and how they weigh it in their mind.

When you need hardware, such as screws, the biggest decision is where to go to get them. The form is determined by the project or repair. For consumer-grade screws, there aren't choices nor do we seek them. You need a drywall screw, you buy the box that most closely matches the quantity you need. There's not much more to it than that. But how could you build value into the screw that would earn a higher price?

You might try premium materials, but that cost would go over most people's heads. Especially for a sunk screw that is meant to be taped, mudded and painted over. The value is not inherent in the product. Like Swiffer, screws are utilitarian. Necessary but not coveted.

A better tack would be branding them, but how? Perhaps looking at the top margin products in Home Depot and licensing the brand name? A consumer won't pay more for a brand they can't identify. But they might pay more for screws branded Milwaukee, DeWalt or Bosch. Milwaukee means power, DeWalt dependability, Bosch innovation. Each of these traits could be passed through to the screw and earn cents per carton. For the consumer that identifies with the values of each specific brand, the extra cost is worth it. But on their own, they remain every bit the commodity discussed earlier.

For almost 20 years, we used Google without even thinking about it. We learned to take any question we had to their simple homepage. It became a screw of the internet. Google identified the job to be done and did it flawlessly. Useful but mostly uninteresting to behold. So dependable, it became an invisible utility. Dominant. Omnipresent. But not *loved* by users. It was utilitarian. Then the brand got emotional. Google introduced a SuperBowl ad about a trip to Paris that leads to love and intrigue, all told through Google searches and results. It was an amazing way to demonstrate how the brand is an emotional medium. From then on the brand was connecting to its specific customer in everything it does.

When they began refining and unifying the brand across its multiple interaction points, something amazing happened. Each modular piece of Google became more valuable and more usable. The familiarity with a core set of menus made new Google software easier to test and adopt. They have converted their massive lead in search and converted it into an army of Google Apps users, a generation who has no need for Microsoft Office. Adding an army of products and features while remaining true to their mission of organizing the world's information.

It hasn't been fool proof, but the look of Google's desktop apps have also translated well to Android. The material design standard makes it easy for Google users to understand the mobile OS and choose it over iOS. The branding has then evolved to include hardware, with the Pixel handset and Pixelbooks popping up and stealing share in their respective categories. The Pixel phone commands a price on par with the flagship iPhone and Samsung Galaxy. Google is able to get away with that for a simple reason: They have trained a generation of customers that their brand is worth it. And they have barely asked consumers to pay them. Most of their services are subsidized by companies. Consumers expect Google services to be free or cheap. But the Pixel is the first time the brand has been specific and worth it, tying all of the value of the services with hardware that makes it sexy.

Remember the Facebook phone or the Amazon phone? Those were not well received by consumers. Those products were rare failures by successful companies. Why? Because the companies had not earned the right to offer that product. The right? you ask. This is commerce; of course they have the right to sell whatever product is within the law by investing their financial and labor assets to develop the product. What they had not earned was the right to assume their specific consumers believed their respective brands translated to that device.

Unlike Google, they hadn't built the brand that could translate into consumer hardware. They are both powerhouses in what they do, but overtaking a user's preferred device just isn't happening. The Amazon Fire Phone was priced comparably to an iPhone, and it should not have been price so high. When the Fire phone launched, the brand was purely transactional, à la Swiffer. At that point, no one considered Amazon a hardware company and already had many good options when it was introduced.

Since the failure of the Fire in 2013, Amazon has returned to hardware. The Amazon Echo has become a success, due in part to its interesting software, Alexa. The voice software helps complete tasks such as shopping on Amazon, search the web, play music and more, and does it at least as well as Apple's Siri. This hardware makes more sense to consumers as it relates to specific customers because it is helping them accomplish tasks similar to those that Amazon might. It just does it in a different way.

Why did the Fire phone fail? Was it truly a bad value or priced too high? The phone *was* short on features and high on cost. Prospective customers did not come out and buy it but that does not mean from a numbers perspective it was entered incorrectly in the marketplace. More likely, it reflects the value Amazon's specific customers put on the service and their understanding of the ways the brand connects to their lives. Especially at the time the Fire launched, Amazon probably saw something most consumers did not: The world was moving to mobile. They recognized that mobile traffic to their properties was increasing every month and saw the threat from Apple and Google owning close to 100% of the on ramps through their mobile OS dominance.

It seems Amazon misread an important aspect of their customer and mobile traffic. At this time, they still had an audience of value shoppers. Before Prime, they had trained customers to come to Amazon largely for deals. Second, they should have recognized that the increasing number of people coming to Amazon properties via smartphones were already used to high quality features and services. Fire matched on price but fell short on experience.

And now with Alexa, Amazon has a personified relationship that is earning value and commanding higher prices. People turn to Alexa to solve problems and though Alexa is artificial, 'she' is more responsive and helpful than the customer service representatives of many other companies. The company has already been able to use the foothold created by the Echo to launch new versions incorporating screens. These occupy a slightly higher price point, but they are a hedge against mobile phone occasions. With an Echo Show, users may turn to that for what may have been an Android occasion in the past.

Amazon controls that traffic and can monetize it (though they haven't so far). They created a device that is priced right, that allows them to control the experience from end to end. The Echo Show is sitting on the counter, awaiting a request. And this, at a time when both Android and iOS have acknowledged too much phone use may not be beneficial and are actively helping users monitor and be aware of their usage. Amazon is there to catch those extra uses. At under $200, the Echo devices are yet another gateway to Amazon's vast customer base, but a move up in price. Like many of

Amazon's services, they invest margin in the early going to build a market, and take price later only when they have a dominant position in the market.

With the Fire TV stick, Prime, the Echo (and Echo Show and Spot) and Alexa, the Amazon brand has moved into more service-oriented territory that builds this connection with customers. Their interaction has become immersive, positioning them to be able to successfully introduce higher priced items based on the emotional expectations and trust consumers have granted.

Voice also abstracts the interaction and creates separation from the slick products and UI of Google and Apple. They recognized a gap in their business and made major moves in product and branding to address that gap. This helped soften competition from two behemoths and move them up the value chain to a position that earns them more margin and consumer attention. In this way, they are also providing more value to their customer. What could not you go to Amazon to accomplish in the US? Very few things.

The failure of the Fire phone has a lot to do with changing technology and markets—factors way beyond the brand. But we can look to commodity products for an example of how branding can affect market price and value. In 1987 the National Pork Board introduced a mass media campaign to promote its product. The famous creative, all tagged with *Pork. The Other White Meat* ran on television, print and elsewhere until 2011. It was everywhere.

In 1960, the wholesale price of pork was 25% lower than beef in the US. The retail price of pork was a third as much as beef. 27 years later at the launch of the famous campaign, the wholesale price of pork was around 20% lower than beef and retail was a little closer at 17%. To clarify the math, the price of pork rose comparatively to that of beef by about 5% wholesale leading up to the campaign. But the retail price difference between beef and pork—what consumers were willing to pay—nearly cut in half.

Why? According to research, people felt pork was more complicated to prepare and cook. They worried that they needed more time and effort to produce great meals with pork as the main protein. People responsible for buying and cooking dinner, wanted simple, nutritious meals. They bought more beef and chicken because they understood the value of those two proteins; homemakers knew how to cook them with confidence.

Once the campaign went live, there were millions of TRPs and trillions of impressions intended to drive preference for pork. The campaign set out to increase the value of pork in the grocery store. How? The Pork Board addressed their specific consumer based on an insight into their shopping and cooking habits. The campaign showed traditional recipes with pork in lieu of beef or chicken, along with unexpected ways to use the product. Here is how the particular customer we want to reach can benefit from these specific attributes of our product.

There were celebrity chef endorsements, and amazing food photography and tons of public relations efforts about the health dangers of red meat. Almost 25 years worth of it. Every single execution was paid off with The Other White Meat slogan. The line was intended to position pork against chicken, but the campaign was aimed at closing the gap between pork and beef, the most expensive mass-consumed meat in the US.

How did the campaign work? From 1987 to 2011 the campaign ran until it was replaced with another campaign that still runs today: Pork. Be Inspired. Research conducted by the USDA showed that per capita consumption of pork increased from 45.6 pounds in 1987 to 48.5 pounds in 2003. Per capita beef consumption declined from 69.5 pounds in 1987 to 62 pounds over that same period.

Back to the gap in pricing. During the period of 1987 to 2017, the price of beef rose faster than the price of pork. The wholesale price of beef doubled. Pork increased by about 35% during that time. But there was a more meaningful change. In 1987—pre-campaign—the wholesale price of beef was almost 59% of its retail price while pork's wholesale price was about 57%. After the campaign, pork's retail differential bypassed beef. In 2017, pork now wholesales for under 40% of its retail price. The wholesale value of beef is 47% of the retail value. In other words, grocery stores now sell beef for about twice what they buy it for while customers pay the grocer about 2.5 their investment for pork.

Pork is now a more profitable item for retailers than beef. The campaign affected the brand to the point that the value proposition of pork changed in the mind of specific consumers. So much so that grocery stores want to stock more, and consumers are happy to pay more. This is a remarkable demonstration of the price value of specific branding. Through repetition of the theme over thirty years, The National Pork Board taught their specific customer that pork was an easier, more flexible and more valuable main ingredient creating demand at a new price premium. The primary grocery shopper and cook in the home was convinced that pork was not special. They were educated on how similar (and simple) it could be to prepare, just like the meats they were used to buying. And at first, the shopper was saving money on a replacement for their usual chicken or beef. But over time, they began to value it enough to pay a little more. And a little more. Until the gap was nearly closed. The specific customer was fed the benefits that earned the desired margin.

Price is what it costs. Value is what your specific customer thinks its worth. Make no mistake, a specific brand is the difference between value and price. A meaningful brand makes the retail price feel like a bargain.

As Phil Barden points out in *Decoded,* a brand is what allows a company to charge more. The examples above are good ways to view specific brands using facets to appeal to the consumers' rational side. But we should look beyond that because the most dramatic examples of price elasticity have little to do with rational thinking.

Have you ever gone to a concert? Have you ever decided you didn't want to sit in the upper level of the arena? It is a person's passion for the music or for the performance that lets TicketMaster charge almost ten times more to see Paul McCartney from a lower level (still not the best seats). Paul McCartney's fans are reacting to their love of the songs, but to something bigger. They are reacting to the nostalgia. Who they were when they heard those songs. Maybe a school dance, a wedding. It's worth paying more to relive the glory days, but it isn't rational.

Every other year the Yankees visit Phoenix and I pay more for tickets to a Diamondbacks game that I normally would. The Diamondbacks are the same team they are the night before the series with the Yankees starts and after the Yankees leave town. For three nights, I am interested in the game at Chase Field where the Diamondbacks play because I have been a Yankees fan since birth. Watching the team play connects me to my memories of living in New York, of first dating my wife. It connects me to a lineage of 100+ years of Yankees players and stories. What the tickets cost, I will pay, even if both teams are having bad years.

The Yankees have a strong brand. But is it built on anything rational? Is Paul McCartney, Drake or Cardi B? No, we like it. We buy it. We pay for the tickets.

For our honeymoon, I asked my wife where she wanted to celebrate. She chose Kauai. Was that rational? Google the cost of hotels. I assure it was *not* rational. But what is rational about remote vacation getaways? Yes, the idea of disconnecting is important (though we still had flip phones when I was first married). But the idea of vacations or travel take rationale out of the equation. If you want the experience, you pay the price.

So when a CPG brand determines they will charge more for their breakfast cereal, they have to figure out what they have done for their specific customer that makes them feel like the decision is an automatic. They have to figure out how to make the customer choose based on a feeling, alone. No additional rationale required. Because it's worth it.

Specific : Adam Pierno

TAKE CARE

This should be the easiest place to understand the importance of being specific. Where emotional response is so immediate. When service is off, there is a first-hand reaction. It can be visceral, like the feeling when a significant other is about to break off your relationship. It just doesn't feel right to either party anymore. The problem in the case of brands is the same as in relationships, one party usually isn't paying enough attention until it's too late.

We know how to take care of the people in our family. Our guests. Our friends. That special treatment usually breaks down when we get too comfortable in those relationships to continue to do it. We don't keep up the special treatment. Is this all that different from customer relationships?

Think about a small business. A local restaurant. When the place opens, the owner who is also probably the manager, takes a special interest in every guest. She understands at that point that every good experience is a referral. She might send them a free drink or appetizer, maybe a dessert. She may personally check in with the guests at the table to see how they are enjoying the place. Taking feedback and tweaking things in front or back of house. When the place gets successful, she checks in a little less. Sends a few less freebies out to the guests. Pays a little less attention to the details.

Details are specifics, after all.

Those are the things your customers love (or hate) about your brand. With no details in the service, there can be no love. It isn't easy to fall in love in a single meeting. People usually learn to love something over time, over repeated exposure to details or service. The bits that are baked into the service that customers get to experience every day are what makes them come back to experience it again the next day. They may even forgive bad service on a single occasion, if they have received great service repeatedly in the past.

What is service? Service is how the product gets from the company to the customer. It is how the problem gets solved. Service is not the fact that the thing happens. It is the style with which those simple things are executed. The very manner in which food is brought from the kitchen or coffee is poured. Those details tell a story.

Theaters illustrate how service expectations have changed. In the golden age of cinema, going to the movies was a major event. The red carpet was out for everyone. The visit was as special as the film. A theater had a custom marquee with blinking bulbs over it. The staff wore formal suits with hats and white gloves. It was closer to fine dining than we remember. Before the film started, red velvet curtains would be pulled apart just like at a live play. People were escorted to their seats by ushers and treated to delicious candies and snacks. Over time, that movie-going experience gave way to teenagers half-heartedly asking if you would like to 'make it a large for just one dollar more.' Sure enough, with a little help from cable, VCRs, Blockbuster, DVDs, fiber optics, Netflix, Sony we learned to stop going altogether. The experience degraded as our home theater and options improved. The service could afford to be mediocre in a world with no competition. Most of us never knew the golden age service to begin with.

It's not necessarily a drop in service that leads to a behavior change. That is important. Context changes around your experience that may make your service suddenly better or worse. When over a period of ten or fifteen years consumers go from captive audiences to having dozens, then hundreds, then infinite video options available on demand. They are going to be more and more incented to stay at home.

When a bank like Monzo becomes available and removes all the flaws and friction in consumer banking, suddenly people start noticing the flaws in the experience at their own bank. And when they call a Lyft effortlessly and are whisked to their destination, they begin to wonder why other services are not just as simple. Context changes expectations across the board, even beyond your core category. If you are thinking specifically, you come with an understanding of the services and experiences your customer loves to help shape your own in comparison. How easy is it for a customer to get their task done? How is this company making it easier or more interesting to get the task done with them?

It is important to become familiar with the service and experience of your competitive set, of course. But anyone your customer interacts with is a competitor in a sense. They are a point of comparison to your service or offering.

The word "service" is more than loaded. It implies a business in which customers pay for another person to perform an action for them. A haircut, an oil change, a cocktail, your taxes. There is a person who you speak with, and that person completes the assignment. Software has become a service, so if you're running a Midas franchise, you now compete with Gmail from an experience standpoint. Go try to book an oil change on *Midas.com* and guess how that comparison is treating Midas. Their business is 75 years old and has nothing to do with software of personal computing, but they have a scheduling tool. Now they are compared to cutting edge technology from Google, Microsoft and anyone else with a calendar on their website.

As an outsider to Midas's technology operation, it appears that they have no idea this is a problem. That's a crime. Not because the software is not great. That is forgivable. There is really no excuse for not being aware of the age and sophistication of your customer base. No excuse for not performing an ongoing audit of your customers emails to determine what sort of stack they are using. A comparison of the vehicles they bring in for work should tell the brand what they need to know about the ways their customer interacts with technology and setting a baseline.

A customer doesn't see the shop. Doesn't meet most of the staff. Doesn't understand most of the certifications and paperwork that goes into keeping the franchise current and up to date. Customers do not know if the tools are proprietary or standard. A customer of Midas, or most other service businesses, sees the person at the desk, the agent. The brand must understand how agents need to fit in to the comparative professionals their specific customer is speaking with at other businesses. Every encounter should be thought about like a call to a customer support line.

They call a number provided by the brand. An 800 number printed on a credit card, for example. Or on the website or email signature. It is the expectation that a question or problem will be resolved for the customer. And they have used the contact information provided by the company. For this reason, agent blending is mandatory. The person that takes the call should be able to solve their problem, not make it worse. Customers do not want to be transferred. They did not want to make a phone call in the first place. Customers want an answer. Usually a specific answer to a specific question. Isolating tasks into departments creates a problem for customers and agents who want to help. Nothing is more frustrating that an inability to communicate.

Locksmiths are victims of the service trap. Because they stay at par within their category, they are judged on perfection in execution only. Remember, brands that provide the Zappos level of service and care get no extra points. That is table stakes. Zappos is famous for empowering people to solve customer problems—to do whatever is needed to make the customer happy. Once they began to perform heroic feats for customers, the tide rose around all other brands. Yet so many have failed to rise with the tide. They barely meet minimum expectations, nevermind the high-water mark set by Zappos.

Airlines are in an unfairly pressurized situation from a service perspective. People call with emergencies and hope for miracle solutions. Tornadoes are running through the flight path, but the traveler still needs to make it to the wedding they are flying home to attend. Added time on the phone with an agent can lead to missed potential solutions for the traveler. In cases like canceled or delayed flights, customers are on edge and agitated. They expect the airline app, desk or phone agent to magically solve their problem immediately. Often, they may know their problem has no solution, but the app is still expected to stop a hurricane or a system-wide software outage that is delaying hundreds of flights.

Zappos and brands like Nordstrom did not earn the reputation of being great customer service organizations because they never got things wrong. Those reputations came from handling tough situations with grace and making the customer feel like someone cared about their problem. They used something critical to strategy and user experience: empathy.

Empathy in customer service is not merely thinking about the state of mind of a customer at a particular time in the customer journey. It is planning for that state of mind and arming agents and technology to respond in a way that will address that pre-loaded emotion. When a person gets shoes in the wrong size, they are annoyed but probably not furious. They aren't panicked in this case. But when they are hours away from a rehearsal dinner at which they are intended to give a speech, they are panicked when their flight is delayed or they miss a connection.

During a social listening engagement for an airline we discovered a deep drop in sentiment over a single day span. For those uninitiated in social intelligence jargon, sentiment refers to the amount of positivity or negativity in the comments and conversations people make about a given topic. When studying brands, sentiment fluctuates as people engage with the brand and post comments. Typically, sentiment had been steady and above average— way above average for a consumer airline. Then there was the mysterious drop. When we reported to the brand we asked about the drop. We learned that it coincided with the date that their reservations system went down. Hundreds of flights were canceled. People were temporarily stranded. And angry. Boy, were they angry.

Sentiment dropped to just about the very bottom of the well. People took to social and travel sites with their gripes. But we could actually chart the recovery the airline made by mapping the sentiment over the next day period. Almost as if each re-booked passenger posted something positive, sentiment bounced back up hour after hour. When the whole episode was over, sentiment was higher than it was before the system outage.

The airline did such a good job of being empathetic that they won people over. No longer angry, they posted compliments about the customer service agents who were bending over backwards to help get them to where they needed to be. Many of the comments focus on agents 'understanding,' 'being there' and wanting to help.

Customer service based on empathy means service that expects a customer's question or issue. *This has been thought through and we know why you might be confused. We are happy to help explain.* This is the equivalent of taking the thorn out of the elephant's paw. The angry customer has missed a connecting flight. For example, the first thing they hear is a sigh from the agent. Perhaps the agent has gotten four straight challenging calls on this same issue. The customer's panic is turned into anger or frustration. But if they hear the friendly voice of an agent, patiently listening and offering to find a solution, the customer is disarmed. They are now ready to accept help or alternative solutions.

This is true of apps and digital touchpoints as well. Many websites and apps offer 'live chat.' A customer is greeted by a picture of a human offering to answer questions or point them in the right direction. Very often, clicking on that chat widget leads to frustration right away. For example, the user is having trouble finding an answer and opens the chat: 'Where do I find this feature?' But instead of a response from Julie the smiling agent in the picture, they get a canned response saying live chat isn't currently operating, offering to send the request as an email. What? Or a gray note shows up that says 'Typical response time is 20 minutes.' Seriously? Re-read what comes next: If you call something live, it must be live. Anything less is the setup for an epic tweetstorm.

No one sets the expectations with live chat except the brand. Instead of a chat widget with Julie's picture, just turn that into an email icon. Turn it into a question mark. Or better yet, have Julie (or whoever will do the best job of helping your customers) actually be there to respond when her picture is featured on the bottom right of the website or app. If Julie is not available live, do not offer live chat. Reading this, it seems ridiculous, I know. Pay attention to the next few sites on which you see live chat. Click on it and watch how often this absentee customer service is presented. It is almost as if brands think that just offering customer service is the same thing as solving customer problems to build loyalty.

The urban legend of the Nordstrom employee taking back snow tires from a customer as a return is the foundation of how their service built that brand. Service is more than answering questions and taking back products you may not even sell. Service is your brand. Service is where your brand meets your customer. Fail at service with a customer and track how long that relationship lasts.

Service is the proof of your commitment to your best customer. Everyone is your competition in service.

After a recent move, we signed up with a new home internet provider. During my brief window of interest, I noticed ads that proclaimed the brand (which I won't name in print) as innovative, affordable and customer-centric. The company did not last one month into my customer agreement. What went wrong?

The system was installed smoothly, the technician took his time and answered our questions. Everything worked great. Two days later, the system dropped off. When I called customer service, I was transferred from agent to agent. Each had a suggestion that did not involve their company's help. I called back and requested a technician simply come back out and take a look at the system, offering that we may have knocked something loose. By this time, I was impatient with the service.

After being transferred amongst a half dozen agents, I asked the next one to connect me with whoever could cancel my account (which they also messed up). During my nearly week-long battle, the company offered to coach me through power cycling my modem about a half-dozen times, to send me a link to a piece of hardware on Amazon, to sell me a second router and annual contract on top of the one I had just signed up for. They threatened to cancel my service or to send me to collections if I opted to cancel. But they never addressed my simple request: please help. I chose your company, and we are off to a rough start. I'd like to work this out. Could you please send a technician out to take a look?

Needless to say, that company is not Zappos or Nordstrom. They do not have the specific mindset of a company that predicts the challenges of its customers and has answers at the ready. And that brand is almost certainly not breaking records with its Net Promoter Score.

Since we now think of service differently in relation to digital products, exchange of data becomes another important factor. We understand when we use products and apps like Facebook, Spotify or MTailor that those companies are pulling data from every tap on the screen to learn our preferences. Some of those preferences are used to shape future engagements and features. Spotify does a good job of passively tracking listener selections and preferences to provide daily and weekly mixes based on their taste. Facebook has been built on understanding us so well they serve us ads that appear as though they must have been listening to our conversations outside the platform (which they vehemently deny).

With most digital services, we volunteer to share this data in exchange for the information we want on demand (Google) or for a better service later (Netflix). We understand this exchange and we are good with it.

But in a live retail environment, we are confounded. It is unpleasant. And it is not immediately clear why we are being asked to provide this data. Radio Shack has long since folded, but it was among the first brands that had agents ask for a zip code with each live purchase. There are still a few that ask for this or something like it. CVS Pharmacy asks for your loyalty card with every purchase to provide you with a ridiculously long receipt that may or may not include a single relevant coupon on it.

If you are a service brand, explain the data exchange to your customers. Or better yet, make the benefits clear so customers understand implicitly, and appreciate the ways in which their experience is improved. So often, we dial into an 800 number and the automated system asks for our account number, date of birth, last transaction amount or the last four of our social security number. Then, an agent gets on the phone and asks us to verify each of those items. *To repeat them.* After providing that litany of information twice, we have earned the right to ask for help. Sometimes, we get some.

Digital brands succeed here because the data they collect seamlessly (some would argue a bit too seamlessly) improves the customer's experience. The brand becomes more useful, fun or engaging. Live retail brands miss when they ask for information without clarifying for the customer why. Remember, the question that feels odd at the counter gets compared to the frictionless experiences of digital brands. Consumer context means all service is compared to the best service. Specific means your service is always relevant.

L.L. Bean is famous for being available for customers at all times. Customers can get an agent on the phone in under a minute, and get an email reply in under an hour. Until last year, they guaranteed items for life; allowing customers to return items decades old for a replacement. They make it easy for their customers to do business with them.

Cosmetics darling Glossier started with the co-founder asking women what products they loved and what they wish they could find; then filling the void with their own line of products. Because the company started with blogs and social media closely engaged with customers, they kept this spirit going as the company grew.

Their team of agents, who they refer to as editors, bridge the customer service and marketing teams. They follow up directly with customers after orders via email or social media to ask how about product and service satisfaction and recommend new products for their next order. Customers with an issue often hear from a proactive editor before they are even ready to contact the company. The roots of the company—what built it from the ground up—is simply asking for customer input and feedback. Keeping that spirit alive continues to make Glossier grow.

Service is a funny thing. As a rule, promising exceptional service is the best way to undermine the quality of the service a customer or guest is about to experience. Building expectations tends to create a goal that is not possible for the brand. Zappos was lauded for its service by the initial, specific customers who appreciated it right up until it became expected. Then, the focus moved to letdowns instead of surprise success.

Users figured out that ridesharing apps were an amazing upgrade from phone calls to taxi dispatch. The specific users the apps were created for. They so enjoyed the upgraded experience, they told people about the apps and the boom was on. Now that the market has become saturated, the quality of service provided is expected. No regular user opens the app filled with awe when the ride arrives. Instead, people take to Twitter to complain that cars are further away than the app had said, or that the car smells funny, or the driver made them late.

The phrase "surprise and delight" has become a lazy cliché. The idea of it is still relevant, however. People get spoiled. They become accustomed. The novel becomes the standard. If the broadband Wi-Fi anywhere slows down (or God forbid, disconnects) people flip out like the end-times have arrived. Ten years ago, there was no Wi-Fi anywhere near as fast or dependable, nor any devices to use on it. If it slows down to something short of ludicrous speed, we lose our minds.

You may be reading this and thinking, these aren't examples of a lapse in personalized service. They are just bad service. I argue that personalized service may not scale for all companies; it may be a pipe dream. Today, people don't expect it, anyway. But bad service is inexcusable. Putting your customer to work, or into awkward situations does not make them feel understood or heard. The brands with excellent service raise the standard for us all.

The idea of surprise and delight was born of this tension. The basics become standardized and customers no longer appreciate them. Companies do the basics, but brands find ways to make customers happy. Whatever that is. Being specific means to bring the details that your customer will notice, appreciate and talk to someone about. To make service personal.

Specific : Adam Pierno

IMPRES-SIONS

The median age in the US is 37.8. The average American makes about $48,000 per year, spends about two hours on social media a day, watches over 30 hours of television per week and reads four book per year. On average they are 17 pounds overweight and exercise 17 minutes a day. They have 11 alcoholic beverages per week and most likely work in retail. The most common American name is James (James Smith to be specific). The most common female name is Mary.

This person doesn't actually exist. They are the statistically average American based on the US Census, Pew Research and other sources. Does this sound like the person you need to reach for your company to turn into a brand? Using media to reach the average consumer will reach this person. Media is all about averages and indices. Playing odds. Selecting media is making bets. Choosing the most watched programs or listened to station, on average, produces an audience something like the above.

When programmatic media buying came on the scene, it was lauded for its self-optimizing efficiency. And it can be great for that purpose. Way down in the tunnel, driving CPA down. Generating more actions per impression and figuring out ways to find more users who will do the same across a set of publishers. It can be a fantastic tool. But programmatic hasn't been developed to be a tool for branding. Is that a function of the methodology or a function of the operators?

Programmatic media buying steers towards a given response. Often a click or something further downstream like a specific conversion point. In the wonderful world of broadcast television, where there is no true direct response, branding is measured by a combination of impressions leading to recall, then to increased awareness and understanding.

So far television has not been able to offer true programmatic options. The intended target don't impact the buy even if they take the advertiser's desired response. Theoretically, digital programmatic should be amazing at delivering brand video to our specific prospect. And in fact it is. A programmatic campaign has trouble improving without response, and so tolerating a video (i.e.., not skipping it) is viable from the mindset of television buying but does nothing to improve future targeting and CPM against your prospect.

Branding is a difficult task for media today because converting in brand terms can take a long, long time. It is much different than converting a lead form or e-commerce sale. Both meaningful outcomes and each part of building a brand, but neither a clear indication of brand building.

As I said at the outset, specific doesn't mean small. Knowing who your best prospect is doesn't mean ignoring the rest of the market. It can't work that way if your company is going to become a big brand. Or even grow. Awareness is still step one. You cannot be selected if you are not known. This has been true since forever but gets forgotten each time the newest version of growth hacking turns up.

Using media intelligently means there is no waste. That doesn't mean you're buying only the exact customers who have raised their hand and opted in. The difference between media waste and specific media is simple. Each time someone sees a message from your company, this impression is an exposure to your brand. It is up to you if that exposure earns attention or is wasted.

There are tons of impressions we ignore daily. The messages that can be ignored have several weaknesses. First, they are not contextually relevant. The message on an outdoor board for a mortgage loan is being served to me at a time when a driver is less likely to be thinking about a home purchase. Second, the message is in no way different from everything that surrounds it. Finally, the message isn't clearly created *for* someone specific. It is often so generalized, it is impossible to pay attention to, even if the off chance the audience intended to.

When we are investing in media, we are making a bet that the person we want to reach will see it. The communication we publish is meant to reach that person with impact. The brand understands the prospect's motivating insight and creates the brand and message based on that motivation. Being specific means making that person feel that the ad was written just for them. Making them feel that you know what they wanted before they knew themselves.

A mere exposure doesn't do this. It is following the laws of awareness too blindly. Just post the logo if all you care about is the impression. If you want to build the brand, no impression is wasted without giving the prospect a hook. A reason to care about the ad and the brand. A hook doesn't have to be a call-to-action (although it might be), it means a reason for the observer to connect and remember the ad or the brand if you can earn their interest. It is something specific that they can store away in their memory for future use. Exposure doesn't do this without relevance. Hooks are whatever about the brand and message that grabs the person and brings them back to it at some future point.

Something about the brand that sticks in the mind of that customer. If it can't be relevant, make it memorable.

Brands have to be clever about the ways they serve exposures to audiences in the awareness phase. They have to reach a broad audience but only in ways and places that make sense for the buyer. The days of buying 200 TRPs during general programming are over for almost all brands. The world of general awareness won't get it done, because it will not have any resonance. It will not have any meaning. And so it won't build the brand.

McDonald's is still one of the largest restaurant brands in the history of the world and thriving by many metrics. They got to the top of the mountain by riding mass media and mass messaging. Their budget affords them the opportunity to continue in mass channels while testing smaller channels to create relevance. For example, they have been the sponsor of the McDonald's All American Basketball program in the US and Canada since the 70's. The players chosen to participate are deemed among the best in the country and are future star players at the college and professional levels.

This program has made McDonald's more than relevant to basketball. It has integrated the brand into the very fabric of the sport. This means that part of the McDonald's brand is basketball. An activity that represents fitness, teamwork, athletic achievement. And for youth players, the game represents something larger about culture. It is as much about the time on the bus and bench as it is about the game.

The brand has become ingrained as part of pre-approval and post-game meals.

Of course the sweeping national sponsorship includes product mentions, promotions and even store locations. There are short-term goals woven into everything the brand does. But for 40 years the brand has reached the young prospect in the same specific phase of their life. With the same interests and aspirations. They have made the brand a core part of their development into adults and educated them about the brand as they were choosing life-long preferences.

Devious, but effective. Generation after generation of Americans bring their children to McDonald's as a treat, thanks in part to this legacy sponsorship.

CONTEXT AND INDEX

Context is everything for a brand. Not necessarily for an advertising campaign. But certainly for a company that aspires to be a specific brand. The brand needs to appear alongside peer brands that I refer to as 'index brands.' Index brands are brands outside of your category that help create the standard for your own brand. For example, if you are a clothing retailer like Forever 21, it helps to identify index brands that can help prospects understand your pricing, styles, and value proposition. Their target consumer is 14-29 year old women. But which segment of that span makes up their best, *specific* target?

Where are these consumers on a relative scale of style - high fashion or casual? Do they prefer long-term, classic choices or are they looking for trendy or fads? Knowing their customer's index brands would go a long way to making product and merchandising decisions that would attract them. For example, understanding what cosmetics their best consumer uses would help them immensely in tailoring their brand tonality and even selecting potential colors and styles for upcoming lines. For a fashion retailer like this, it would help to know their retailer preferences in grocery, club stores and big box. A Walmart shopper is clearly different from a Target shopper. But how does a Costco shopper compare as it relates to fashion?

What restaurant brands do their targets frequent? What kinds of cars do they drive - and which do they aspire to drive? Uber or Lyft? Nike, Adidas or Lululemon? Each of these decisions build the index that can be used to figure out how this brand can behave. People use brands as a shorthand to help define the people they meet. Brands can do the same to build their own.

Once we understand which brands are preferred by our target, we can then study the media they choose and the way they speak to their customers. We borrow styles and ideas from their products, and can learn even more about how to reach them from their media mix. This can be a shortcut to creating a draft of the brand media plan, figure out where the brands they love are and use the index by becoming a part of it.

Context is easier and harder than ever. Digital platforms have made contextual targeting as easy as ever. Facebook and Google allow advertisers to reach people when they are in the market for a given category. Google has a targeting mode called "In market" with categories listed out. This is fantastic for lower funnel activities; great for sales. It is a challenging way to build a brand.

Programmatically or otherwise, context becomes a problem when we look at what is surrounding a message. Sometimes, when I'm watching television, a commercial pod will be full of ads for catheters or feminine hygiene products. There is nothing wrong with these products, but I am not in the market for either. It makes me question whether I'm meant to be watching this show. I will actually rethink my interest in the show based on the relevance of the ads, and not the other way around 'Am I watching the wrong show or is the brand?'

Those are innocent circumstances. What about when your message is served up on a website next to something horrible. Programmatically, an ad for a children's' product on a website with adult content. Or ads served alongside terrible news that creates dissonance for the brand. Accidental in most cases, but it can be damaging. And some smart-ass always shares a screenshot on Twitter for all to see.

What about in the deeply polarized climate of today's political discourse? Advertising on any news programming is a minefield when people are ready to boycott advertisers of any story that voices an opinion they disagree with. This is a real problem since news is content that attracts viewers, it has an audience, but is dangerous to brands when the content can turn on its head in an instant. When a host like *Today*'s Megyn Kelly stumbles into her controversial opinions on black face, live content gives a producer nowhere to turn for respite but to a commercial break. Great. And now a word from our sponsor. Your brand gets lumped in with the controversy, when you intended to buy the wholesome morning programming.

In a dynamic environment, context can be a nightmare. YouTube for example was revealed to host thousands of videos using children's characters in shocking scenarios such as torture in a dentist's office. Bizarro versions of Spider-Man, Elsa and others pop up in awful scenes. Legitimate children's content hosted on the site by verified brands and producers was just a few clicks or autoplays away from these terrifying videos. Journalists began to report on the number of extremist videos and conspiracy content on YouTube. Suddenly (and rightfully) brands advertising or posting videos on the platform began to pay attention to brand safety. The very idea that the context can improve or corrupt a brand.

Of course, the average American rejects extremist content. She does not want to watch violence and avoids related videos. By a combination of clicking and autoplay, she ends up watching a car ad, followed immediately by a violent extremist video. She is upset, and has an impression of the car in the context of the violent content surrounding it. This begins a challenging question. For example, let's suppose a person searches for extremist content. They want to watch it. They may enjoy it for one reason or another. If this person who seeks out the content and enjoys it sees the same car ad, is the context positive or negative?

This is troubling for the brand who wants to have a positive brand image (in a simple moral framework) but ends up aligned with or symbolic of what is negative to the mainstream. Context matters.

These types of contexts may be unavoidable in a digital world in which limitless channels limit the extent to which content can be assessed. As we discussed, awareness must be constantly built. The brand must communicate wherever the specific customer is found.

How often do you get married? Odds are, not very often. Most weddings traditionally happen in Q2, and in 2018 Q3. Yet David's Bridal has more than 300 stores in the US that need to sell dresses and accessories all year round. They advertise throughout the year to maintain awareness always. As with everything, people work at their own pace. Brides plan weddings at differing speeds and with different goals. Some are planning before they are even engaged, anticipating. Some have the involved help of their partner. Some are planning at the very last minute.

David's is an affordable option for brides and bridesmaids. This is an exception in the wedding industry. Most other brands and designers focus on luxury and premium experience to exploit the 'once in a lifetime' aspect of the event and the way American women have been taught to think and feel about their wedding. The brand had been messaging through traditional channels like television and print with little lower funnel support. They were aiming for broad awareness in bridal content. This was missing the point of being specific. Mass media is great for awareness but poor context can hinder specific understanding.

The brand got away with it until fast fashion brands began offering low-priced dresses and accessories for brides and their wedding parties. Brands like ASOS, H&M, Missguided, Reformation, Topshop and (many) more have jumped in to the category with affordable options. Fast fashion brands have a reputation for trendy, good-looking attire that is meant to be worn in the moment and affordable.

David's had occupied a space that was essentially the only national option for low-cost wedding dresses, but messaged it as a part of the industry. Advertising alongside wedding content like *Say Yes To the Dress* and *Modern Bride* magazine hurt their mass awareness. By claiming to be a part of the mainstream wedding business, David's failed to reach a specific customer, instead appealing only on price. To make matters worse, when the brand looked to expand awareness through brand partnerships, they became a part of Walmart weddings. That index brand should paint a picture. Brides looking for an affordable option had a choice, but brides and families with more money to spend were turned off by the brand.

Fast fashion brands have entered the category as an antidote to the industry, not merely as a low-cost option. Everyone who has planned a wedding knows that adding the words 'wedding' or 'bridal' increase the cost of any item or service by x%. Fast fashion has entered the world of weddings as an outsider, appealing to a specific bride who wants a stylish gown and does not believe in paying a premium. In other words, the bride who does not see the need for a designer dress and doesn't want David's. David's left a gap in the market through product and messaging, but unintentionally reinforced their own weaknesses by their approach to media.

By advertising to women who were in the planning phase, they were being efficient. It would be difficult to argue against that strategy, especially in an event-based retail business with hundreds of brick and mortar locations to feed. But by serving the message of the discounted option, they were not being wise. Price points are not something associated with weddings, but value could have been communicated in many ways. Bridal content focuses on the unique, the special, the custom. In other words, the antithesis of David's: the mass market, chain store of weddings. This context created a trap for the brand by backing themselves into a corner against luxury, premium and dream-fulfilling options. David's positioned the brand as a discount option to women who believe their wedding is a time they are justified to splurge. The combination ruled out a higher-end audience. It created a problem for the audience they got, many of whom yearned for a premium designer product, but felt that they had traded down by settling for David's. The brand's media plan put them into a slot that felt like an advantage, but turned into an albatross when fashion retailing shifted. This was created by their business model, the brand messaging and the shift in consumer taste and preference for fast fashion, but accelerated by the context the brand created for itself. A brand error, made worse through media.

Instead of focusing on buying in the highly competitive spaces that forced its brand position, David's could have focused on building out a media plan based on the index brands. What other brands do David's best, and most satisfied customers love? What other brands do they shop regularly? Finding those brands and mapping their media footprints would have provided a rough plan for reaching their specific customer and building affinity.

As discussed earlier, media is getting ever more fragmented. With the limited ability to reach the millions of people we once did with prime time broadcast television, it is tempting to favor precise targeting over reach. *If I can't reach everyone, I'll just target the people who like my page.* But this is flawed because that audience can't grow without being introduced to the brand. And how are they introduced to the brand? Often by ads. The idea of being specific is not to be prescriptive. Specific brands have a point of view, but remain accessible to those who are attracted to a given facet of the brand. Therefore, brands need to buy a broader audience to expose them to the facets of the brand.

Media still allows for the reach and frequency required to create lasting awareness. It is just getting more difficult to put together the number of impressions required and more challenging to avoid the traps. Targeting is a trap when it comes to awareness. How do I know? Pop culture. Yes, summer movies are created for a demographic. They are advertised to a demographic. But when they hit, it is because they win over people outside that audience and pull more people into the theater. Hence the reason every movie seems to be a remake or based on something we are already familiar with. The advertising doesn't have to educate consumers about why to see the film, it just has to keep reminding them to buy a ticket.

Pop music works the same way. Record labels worked extremely hard to guide the creation and programming of radio formats. This was done to organize listeners into groups that were prepared to consume particular types of music. Then digital audio came along and people were able to discover endless types of music at little risk. Country fans could explore the Outkast catalogue. Speed Metal fans could test K-Pop. Listeners were able to self-select into their own unique tribes and take in the music they like the best. Admittedly, there aren't many Body Count fans with BLACKPINK in their collection. But in order to enjoy it, they had to be exposed to it.

But how? The music industry barely advertises individual artists or tracks. Recommendations. We have seen the growth of the influencer bubble over the past five years due to the power of recommendations. At first influencers seemed to hold sway over people as gurus. Brands thought that an influencer could legitimately persuade followers to buy something. According to Collective Bias, 70% of millennial consumers are influenced by the recommendations of their peers. And something like 92% of millennials trust peers over brands.

No kidding. This has always been true, it just hasn't been quantified. Influencers are valuable. But they don't hold peer influence. A person holding up 20 different products over 18 Instagram posts isn't believable as a spokesperson, and they aren't viewed as a peer. What influencers do have is a media following. They serve impressions. Ironically, we have seen that bigger influencers begin to lose influence as their following grows. Why? Because they become a brand. And people don't trust brands as much as they trust peers. So buying a post from a Kardashian will get you more impressions, but it won't be viewed as a peer recommendation. It is viewed as a celebrity endorsement, the same as Cindy Crawford in a Pepsi ad. That doesn't make it a bad decision. Does adding either woman make a beverage more drinkable? It doesn't matter because both make the advertising message more watchable by the specific target and people who may be more interested in the celebrity than the soft drink. A celebrity is a shortcut to attention in the same way intellectual property is. A consumer who recognizes it, marks it mentally in their mind.

Somehow, influencers have become associated with social and digital marketing. Which makes no sense since spokespeople have existed before radio. Posters and newspaper ads had celebrities. Radio ads had celebrities endorsing products. Television has had a love affair with celebrities, with the very first shows being entirely sponsored by brands. Celebrity was originally used to drive broad awareness. In the influencer world it is often used to reinforce that interest among people who already signaled interest in the brand in the first place.

The signals with social and digital take the form of metrics. The question with media and metrics is - what is the value of the information they provide? To begin with, upper funnel metrics have been consistently challenged and proven false from even the biggest and most trusted providers. Viewability and ad fraud have meant that ads have run less, been more invisible and viewed for shorter durations than Google, Facebook and hundreds of ad networks have reported.

Everything in digital media has been gaining importance for two reasons. First, the use of digital media is trying to keeping pace with the amount people are incorporating digital into their lives. Digital is taking over media plans because digital is taking over our work and leisure. Second, there has been a hundred years of advertising using gut and estimated guesses at what works and what doesn't. Digital offers metrics and measurement. People love evidence. We flock to things that can be proven. And so marketers continue to invest in digital, paying a premium for the metrics they cannot get from television, radio, print or out of home.

That data grows and grows, creating the targeting trap of media.

Data tells a story, or rather, people use data to tell a story. In our jobs, we want to tell a story about success to protect our position. We focus on positive metrics that demonstrate how good we are at our jobs. A marketer's job is to successfully bring the product to market. Sales metrics are a good measurement. Using media, there isn't always a direct metric to measure that for brands without e-commerce or digital conversion. So impressions gave us a way to measure against traditional media. Clicks gave us a way to measure an action. Likes measured, uh, engagement, I guess?

For brands playing in digital without e-commerce those metrics tell us something about the brand. Or at least about the content. We can see what they responded to. To be clear, we can see the number of people who reacted from the subset of those who were exposed to it. The trap is that we fall in love with the small response from those who are most likely to react to the brand (often existing customers) and begin a cycle of repeating similar content.

Like trained seals, we want the fish so we do the trick again. Students who constantly ask questions like 'Will this be on the test?' are proven to have a shallower level of learning. So it goes with brands. Preparing for only the metrics that can be measured. Only what's on the test. And the brand stays locked in a loop. Why? The metrics said so. When everyone was chasing page Likes, we believed we were growing our audience and this made sense for specific brands. Recruit more people into our club. But once social platforms started toying with organic reach (it is currently below 2% on Facebook) growing Likes no longer mattered. Now, it was buying more impressions. Which is absolutely fine but ironic because that is how we bought traditional media. But a traditional television spot that reaches a hundred thousand people can't be clicked on, and therefore can't show up in a dashboard. Some now consider it less valuable.

Social media is powerful for focused targeting, which works in the specific framework by sharing brand facets. Campaigns, featuring short messages to help illustrate facets to prospects, move people from awareness to understanding. Plus social and digital platforms like Adwords allow brands to target by intent, to show that David's Bridal ad not just when the prospect has announced they are engaged, but to begin showing the prospect David's Bridal ads when *her friends begin getting engaged*. So the brand can position itself based on its facets while the prospect is forming her opinion and not when she is competitively assessing the entire category.

The metrics for this type of pre-emptive brand building may not look great. A woman not currently planning a wedding is not likely to click on anything. The campaign metrics won't knock anyone over. But unaided awareness in the bridal category is a huge asset. Most wedding brands have been obscure to non-brides, save Vera Wang and major design houses. Following trends and obeying the dashboard can remove the competitive leverage from a brand. Having a brand point of view that meets your specific target creates a media strategy that can move markets.

Specific : Adam Pierno

STAYING SPECIFIC

The first *Friday the 13th* movie was derivative. It was a take-off on the surprise success of *John Carpenter's Halloween*. The production team behind *Friday the 13th* copied the beats of *Halloween* as they interpreted them, and pasted them into a film they knew a similar audience would line up to see.

Critics reviewed the original as a film, commenting on the story, performances and direction, though the notices were not good. The second *Friday the 13th* was more derivative, building off the ideas in the first and adding more of what the producers felt the audience liked best (and less of the few things critics liked). When the third *Friday the 13th* was released, the template was cast. Though the third film changed by introducing the iconic hockey mask, the rest of the film was a carbon copy of the most titillating and shocking elements of the prior two.

There have been twelve *Friday the 13th* films. Needless to say, they aren't getting smarter. Over the first ten films, the audience got relatively smaller or remained flat for each one. The films satisfied their specific customer but never evolved (with the exception of the hockey mask). Because they picked up the same elements episode after episode, they never recruited new customers. They never gave new people a reason to rethink the brand. I know what these films are and I don't like it. Box office receipts did not increase for *Jason X* (in which the killer goes to space in the year 2455, yes seriously). The new setting did not convince moviegoers that the story would be any different.

What did boost ticket sales? *Freddy vs. Jason,* the combination of two characters of derivative horror franchises that had been spiraling down to satisfy their same small fan bases. Finally, something new happened in the film that gave people a reason to believe the story would be different. The result? *Freddy vs. Jason*, the eleventh installment of the

Friday the 13th series, earned almost $100 million more than the tenth, *Jason X*. Was it drastically different? Average moviegoers wouldn't be able to tell you anything except the introduction of another major character, because most people had never seen the previous film series in its entirety. There were still helpless teens being stalked by a giant killer in a hockey mask, this time joined by another scary guy with a pointy glove.

Yes, brands can learn something from *Friday the 13th*. Sticking to the formula will produce dependable results. Each film cost a few million to make and yielded a reasonable return. But the audience didn't grow. The producers of each film had to go into the first nine knowing they would make a little money by bringing back the same story elements and the same customers and rarely any new ones. Brands work the same way. Being specific can be viewed as a lid that prevents growth. Brands that do it right know how to recruit new customers and present ways to earn new customers. But others follow the example of film sequels, serving a shrinking audience more of the same and failing to grow.

In 2001, World Wrestling Entertainment bought it's biggest and last rival, World Championship Wrestling. The two companies had been battling on Monday nights through competing cable TV franchises and pay-per-views for a few years. They traded stars and storylines, but ultimately the WWE won out, and immediately shut down WCW and discarded any remnants of the organization save a few of the bigger star performers.

The WWE had bested its final rival, and all who had come before it, through better promotion, smarter deals and stories and talent that appealed to its customer base.

With no big competition, WWE had a monopoly over wrestling if such a thing exists. They control the market for top talent and its development. Professional wrestlers are unicorns. They possess the athletic ability and endurance to perform at a high level (even fake fights take their physical toll) and the charisma of Hollywood actors.

Over the next decade and a half, the WWE enjoyed a golden age, growing revenue and dictating what wrestling fans consumed in the US and much of the world. They told fans who to cheer for, who to boo, who would be champion and who would be the villain. Interestingly, with no competition, fans started getting restless. They started questioning the storylines, and challenging the selection of new talent. They got bored of seeing the same old cycle of character development.

To stay relevant and avoid new competition, WWE hires more talent than it can possibly find time for in its two weekly cable shows. Some of the brightest wrestling talent in the world is on the sidelines waiting for an opportunity to appear on a WWE telecast. The talent they do invest in requires a major investment because of the stakes. They need to make sure that a wrestler like Roman Reigns will 'go over' because there is more than cheers on the line. There is millions in merchandise, toys, video games and licensing. The result of repeated predictable goals for an organization is predictable outputs. WWE is afterall entertainment and to remain on top, it must entertain its specific customers.

Wrestling fans are an interesting lot. I'm going to whisper this next bit, as to not offend them. They all know wrestling is fake. Wrestling fans understand they are watching a violent soap opera. They know punches, dropkicks and codebreakers really don't land. They know archrivals like The Iron Sheik and Hacksaw Jim Duggan were friends outside the ring. For the duration of the show, they ignore the facts and enjoy. And they enjoy on their very specific terms. They want energy. They want surprise. They want a say. They not only want certain wrestlers to win, they want them to win the 'right way.'

With no competitive company, WWE got pretty used to just giving the fans whatever it wanted. This was all fine until another company popped up committed to giving the fans everything they wanted. Actually, it wasn't even a company when it popped up, it was more of a pop up event. *All In* started as a bet on Twitter between personalities on the outs with WWE and a wrestling journalist. They bet each him they could get 10,000 to attend an event and set out to do it. They began to question what it would take to pull 10,000 fans in to a wrestling event.

It turns out, they had access to plenty of information. They watched WWE and planned the opposite. They listened week after week to complaints of the fans of WWE. Every way that

WWE took advantage of its fans and talent, All In was determined to pay it back to fans. What started as a small independent event was immediate lauded as the best wrestling event in years. The show won its 10,000 ticket bet in under 30 minutes by telling the audience exactly what they were going to see.

All In provided the talent that WWE had discarded or would not sign - talent fans love - and put them in familiar situations and matchups. Then, they executed. All In figured out how to reach that specific audience. The people who love the sport of pro-wrestling, not just the WWE. The event was well written, well organized and the wrestlers did everything flawlessly. Fans got surprises. They got the familiar. And they got the familiar surprises they craved but didn't expect to be so well done. All In featured talent from almost all the small wrestling companies in the US and talent from around the world. The organizers got permission from these organizations to use their talent, their technology and their time to put on a show fans loved. Meanwhile, WWE sits on its stockpile like the movie theater telling customers they can't bring their own candy into their showing. While WWE is still dominant, the All In event proved that specific fans are looking for an alternative and rekindled the idea of competition in a category under monopoly rule for years.

How many times has someone told you a terrible, unfunny joke. You wanted to like it but you just didn't. A close friend said "I have a joke for you." You listened. *Nothing.*

Did you go tell someone the joke? No, you probably did not. This applies to everything about being specific. Memes do not spread just because they are recommended by a peer. Songs do not become hits because someone else told you they are good. People do not fill theaters because someone told everyone to go buy a ticket. The introduction to the meme, the song, the film may come from a friend or a peer. Like the joke, if it falls flat, it dies there. For a meme to travel, it has to have the emotional resonance that makes the recipient pass it on.

You might say "I can see why you like that joke, but it is not funny to me." Or some translation for the film, song or meme. When we pass something on, we're endorsing it. We are saying "Hey, look at this thing I found!"

What if the joke was offensive to you? Racist, misogynist, mean or just out of line with your values. Or if it made fun of someone close to you. Would you tell the joke?

Creating a specific brand means building in facets for your best customer to find and love. And choosing facets that someone similar, but not identical can grab a hold of when it finally gets passed to them. Why do action movies have love stories? So people can like them even if they are not interested in things blowing up. Why do most restaurants have kids menus? To make the place more attractive to parents and to kids. Restaurants that focus on adult menus however, are not wrong. They attract people with adult taste, who aren't concerned about a child's response and maybe even hoping to avoid unruly children. A different hook for a different brand and prospect.

WWE figured out what its fans loved over 35 years. From studying their competition and promoting the biggest stars in the world, WWE mastered the art of pro wrestling. But they began to believe they knew better than their customers. WWE believed they could dictate what they should prefer, who they should root for and who would and wouldn't wrestle. They lost their most passionate fans who had stopped sharing the brand and began seeking an alternative.

Lego is one of the most interesting products ever created. The tiny blocks have captured the imagination of kids around the world for decades. During my youth, I spent hours building and rebuilding with boxes of Lego bricks. The sets came with characters that were happy, minimalist and nondescript. The bricks were designed to work as an expandable system so any set could be added to any other and play could grow. As a child this allowed me to stretch my imagination and put them into all kinds of stories of my own creation. For a certain type of kid, seeing Lego meant dropping everything. The toy isn't for everyone, but it is captivating to others.

In the 1990's, Lego sought ways to bring more kids into the fold. The Danish brand began a series of aggressive licensing deals beginning with the biggest of all intellectual property at the time: *Star Wars*. It was a coup. Sales of those first *Star Wars* Lego sets sold in huge numbers marking new growth for the brand. The *Star Wars* movie franchise have been relatively dormant in pop culture before new films arrived at the time of the Lego deal, offering kids a new hook. Now fans of *Star Wars* could enjoy Lego, too.

This lift in sales lead to a spree of licensing over the next two decades. Harry Potter, DC, Marvel, Minecraft, Jurassic Park, Overwatch, etc. Each set had new custom pieces to match the theme and make it special. At first, the deals yielded more growth but over time, sales did not keep pace.

In 2014, Lego began promoting a new series of sets made for girls. Lego Friends was designed to inspire girls to play with the bricks and essentially the toys took the form of Lego doll sets. The minifigures were skinnier and less blocky. They were taller, breaking the scale of the other sets and making it challenging for kids to mix Friends minifigures with other Lego minifigures.

In 2017, the brand fell back and announced the first layoffs in years. What changed? Kids weren't necessarily sold on Lego, they were brought in by things they already liked. The company saw a lot of sales to kids for whom Lego was an accessory to another interest. My son loves Harry Potter, so here is the Hogwarts playset. Some—but not all—converted to Lego fans. When the Harry Potter sets stopped, they stopped buying.

The beauty of the original Lego system was that any brick could be added to any other group of bricks. In a typical set, it would come with directions for how to make a main model, but then offer alternate suggested models inspiring kids to take apart the model and reassemble. But a licensed set offers no alternative. If you are building the Millenium Falcon, you want the Millenium Falcon. Most kids won't take it apart and use the pieces in other ways. The hook brought in customers but changed the brand for a lot of customers. It encouraged less imagination and became a more standard (and more expensive) model kit. It made the toys less 'sticky.' There was no reason to come back and play with it again the next day. For many of these children, it became a toy destined for the shelf, not the floor. That toy does not get played with during play dates, it stays on the shelf. The idea does not get shared. It is not a meme.

Lego Friends was initially met by criticism for pandering to girls and steering the way they should play. But the brand insisted the nuance to the girls' line came from academic and primary research into what girls sought from play. Still, some parents were confused and others put off by the Friends line, which sold strong at the outside. The line and the positioning to girls created a question in the minds of customers—not necessarily the children playing with the toys, but the parents buying them. Why did Lego need to have a special set for girls? The brand had created a new hook, but earned scrutiny and not loyalty from their prospects.

In this way, the brand swelled in size using a new customer to extend. But the gains didn't last because the hooks that were added didn't align with the brand that was built for Lego's specific customer. The net sales and size of the brand are bigger but the growth with most new customers was short lived.

In truth, the licensing partnerships hurt the brand long term. Licensing brought in thousands (millions?) of new customers. How could this be bad? Many of the new customers were only fractionally interested in Lego. As they got more specific (yes, there is such a thing) they brought in more people who were primarily interested in the partner and only a few who maintained interest in Lego. The brand became an accessory to the licensed property. No different than the lunchbox, the Happy Meal toy and the breakfast cereal.

Here is a question. Did Lego need to launch a new brand for girls at all? Could Lego have just begun rolling out the same sets under the Lego banner and let content of the set determine who would buy? On one hand, Lego is Lego. All the sets are meant to add scale and value to previous sets and pieces. On the other hand, the specific brand, Lego Friends created a banner for a new specific consumer. Lego Friends brought in a new specific customer. Though this new customer came with a lower lifetime value than their core customer so far, they have proven in part to be recurring customers who understand the modular nature of the sets. An examination of retail spaces would likely show that Lego earned new space in the 'girls' toy section when Friends launched, although retailers like Walmart and Target have been breaking down the walls between gendered offerings now.

Unlike WWE, Lego was expanding the brand by adding entry points. They were seeking ways to invite new customers and using data to create new hooks. As WWE became a monopoly, the company failed to innovate, at least according to critics. They were adding new ways to extract more revenue per customer such as more pay-per-view events and a streaming video subscription service. But the belief that they were giving fans what they wanted lead to giving them reruns of the same ideas. This added up to less for fans to get excited about, and no new reason for fans to watch or recommend, while making room for a new entrant in the space.

This idea—to create a specific story for a single customer—is, of course, an oversimplification. That is an understatement to be sure. The earlier example of washing detergent has to appeal to a broad set of users to sustain any semblance of relevance. Tide has evolved with American consumers and found simple and innovative ways to build new hooks that invited a growing audience to choose the brand over competitors.

Only a few years ago, they introduced a portable version of the product that had broad appeal but reinforced the brand value they have been crafting with their specific customer for 70 years. The Tide pen builds on the efficacy of the Tide brand.

Of course, the pen adds a new dimension that invites a new type of customer and expands the boundaries of Tide. Since the brand's inception, Tide has existed in one place. A single room of the home—the laundry room. Procter & Gamble did such a good job of training us how to use the brand that it was not possible for Tide to escape the laundry room.

Awareness was maxed out and understanding of the brand tied it firmly to the washing machine. But the Tide pen put the brand in millions of pockets and bags. People were now carrying the brand with them every day. This, along with the launch of Tide Dry Cleaning centers are expanding the understanding of the brand and with it the potential for an already huge brand.

Who is the core customer for Tide? The brand was built on the American housewife. That specific customer who was the center of the home and became a marketing cliché. We understand today that women aren't staying at home doing laundry and watching soap operas and haven't in decades. Wisely, Tide remained true in its core brand communication, focusing on the home and homemaker—whoever they may be today—while uncovering new ways to grow share.

Tide Dry Cleaning centers are a no-brainer of a brand extension, but a huge departure in business model. Licensing the brand name into a franchising model is a risk for Procter & Gamble. Having invested so much time and money in building specific equity means that the expectations consumers have are very high and crystal clear. *I know what the brand does for me, and it has never let me down. It comes in the same dependable format and produces its same dependable results.* But the physical locations introduce a human element, a service element that could help or harm the brand equity.

Both of these extensions speak to the changing shape of the customer for Tide. Awareness is likely not a problem for any adults in the US. But the need to expand understanding and value is critical for Tide. They had taken the core product just about as far as could be expected, especially given the changes to household management and CPG usage. The two products take an opposite end of the spectrum for the cleaning category to expand the brand.

More people take some portion of their laundry out to be cleaned than during the brand's heyday. The Tide Dry Cleaning centers capitalize on an opening in the marketplace. These locations allow people, who are looking for ways to get cleaning done outside the home, to have a branded place with a value they know. Most other cleaners are mom and pop or lesser known organizations that haven't figured out a true position among consumers. Results are mixed, and reliability is not guaranteed. Tide Dry Cleaning centers serve the specific Tide customer along with the working mom, familiar with the brand but looking for help with laundry, as well as anyone looking for a dependable brand to handle cleaning.

On the other side, people are looking for convenience in everything they do. They are looking for small ways to make life easier and limit extra laundry or trips to the laundromat. They might also be looking for quick cosmetic fixes to the regular mishaps that cause stains. The Tide pen makes this possible. It is so simple. It is a wonder it took so long. No other brand could have successfully launched the pen, because no other detergent brand symbolizes dependable clean. The Tide pen works for the specific Tide customer, while leveraging the brand's unparalleled awareness to hook new consumers based on product design. In the center of these two points remains Tide's core brand. Dependable clean. Now, the brand is out in public to be seen and discussed instead of hidden in laundry rooms across the country.

At first, staying specific may be more clear to the brand than it is to the customer. Ford is transforming its lineup of vehicles from economy cars through heavy duty trucks by cutting the production of sedans and small cars entirely, with the exception of their iconic Mustang. They are investing in maximizing profit margins in pickup trucks and sport utility vehicles, self-driving technology and exploring alternate transportation options like scooter sharing services. Their goal is to offer products and services based on the data created and captured by transport and reported by vehicles and smart streets that consumers have not even recognized they want yet.

This is a big bet and Ford believes they know the consumer well enough to push their chips in on this idea. Imagine telling investors you plan to cut half of your product lineup that you have spend billions branding like the Focus or Fusion. Time will tell whether Ford is WWE, seeing dollar signs in higher margin pickup trucks or Tide seeing a marketplace opportunity to take the product out of the laundry room. Being specific does not mean small, and it should act as a limit to potential. The original Tide brand is incredibly specific despite relevance to millions of Americans.

The brand's adherence to its best customers yielded billions in sales of the core product and ultimately lead to the ability to unlock new areas.

To return to horror films, the third *Halloween* film did something unusual for a horror sequel. It left the main character out of the film. Entirely. Michael Myers, the killer from the first two is not in the film at all and neither are any other characters or any of the plot lines. It is an entirely new story leaving behind all that fans of the first two films loved. They bucked the trend of horror franchises re-telling the same story, they earned 60% of box office sales of the second film, and almost an 80% drop in box office from the original film. They squandered the brand awareness they had earned with the first film, something truly original. They failed to offer core customers what they wanted, but also failed to entice new moviegoers to spring for a ticket with their new story. Without a specific customer in mind, they created a product almost nobody wanted.

Specific : Adam Pierno

CLOSING

We have covered a lot of ground, haven't we? Companies exist to fill a market need. But brands exist to serve a specific customer, in a specific way. Brand awareness is necessary to make a brand grow. If it isn't known, it cannot be considered. The brand's specific customer must have an understanding of how to use the brand. When to use it. And maybe, when to *not* use it.

What is a "specific brand?" It is a company that understands who its best customer is and builds everything it says and does around that customer. This may alienate some people who have a different point of view. That is the exact point. The specific brand exists to please its customer, and grows when it can inspire more people to become customers based on that happy group of core customers.

In the restaurant space, we see brands fall away all the time because customers don't know how to use them. They don't know the signature occasion for the restaurant. This is almost always a result of lumbering scale. Look at the casual dining rise and crash. As casual dining grew in the US, the country was carved up into 10-15 distinct brands, each with their purpose. Olive Garden lead the way for Italian food. Outback was for steak. Red Lobster for seafood. Red Robin for hamburgers. Applebee's won out over rivals Friday's and others for the neighborhood pub space. There were lesser rivals that filled in certain spaces and runners-up in each category. It worked because customers in given areas understood when to go to each place because it was divided pretty neatly into turf. These places had a purpose for the guests.

First fast casual (Five Guys, Chipotle, etc.), then delivery services (Postmates, Seamless) matured over ten years and began confusing the matter. Meal kit services appeared on the scene which may have ultimately only served as a fad that reminded people they didn't have to eat every meal out. All of these external forces created pressure on casual dining brands to break down their offering. Outback, Chili's et al began pushing take out, removing their potential experiential edge in the name of traffic. Then they began spinning out fast casual versions of themselves like Red Robin's failed Burger Works brand, further breaking down their value proposition. With each concession, these once giant brands lost sight of what made them what they were.

Who is their specific customer and what did the brand do that they loved. What purpose did they serve for the brand. Like a niche brand, specific brands know how they fit into the market and are never confused. Their customers know exactly how to use the brand and what role it plays in their life.

This year, a well-known casual dining brand offered a new change to their menu. They advertised with national television ads using *That's Amore* (timely!) playing over beautiful slow motion shots of pasta being tossed in sauce. Olive Garden, right? Macaroni Grill? No. It was Applebee's, the neighborhood pub brand. It is apparent that Applebee's has no idea how customers should use their brand. In the past two years, they have remade their kitchens to feature fire grills, offered steaks, pivoted to ribs, then to boutique flavored appetizers and entrées designed to bring in food truck loving millennials. And now pasta. Each of these campaigns has been about a 13-week flight. That's not enough time for a customer to relearn the brand.

Like a horror movie franchise, Applebee's has awareness which is serving as a curse. People know the brand and avoid it because they can't find the hooks that make it relevant to them. But Applebee's is changing the story every three months. For the relative few that try the offer and like it, the offer is gone if they've learn to love it. The brand is blurry from the inside and the outside.

Specific brands serve a higher order benefit for their customers. By filling a unique space in their lives, the brand has a meaning that is conductive. It conducts to brand or line extensions or pivots into new spaces that make sense to the customer. It allows a video game console to change shape. It allows a detergent to become a laundromat.

A brand this specific cannot, by definition, look and sound like everything else. Regardless of channel, a specific brand is immediately identifiable and memorable. It doesn't blend into the category. It doesn't get confused with competitors. It does not take the form of a given platform. Investment in a specific brand means never missing an opportunity to differentiate.

Geico was the first US insurance company to use comedy in its ads. Before Geico introduced the gecko, insurance brands were serious, steadfast, reliable. Mature. Insurance is not a laughing matter. Right? Now laughing is almost standard. Each brand is doing some kind of upbeat joke in their television and video ads. Why? Because it was successful for Geico, increasing policy sales, awareness and NPS.

Thirty years in, and it seems that the first brand to break ranks with a serious, grown up message might have a chance to differentiate. Geico found its specific customer was someone that wanted to save money on their policy and

didn't want to worry about potential negative outcomes—
the reasons we buy insurance. They wanted the comfort of
having coverage without dwelling on why you might need it.
Allstate uses Dennis Haysbert (called internally the Voice of
God) as their serious spokesman while hedging with their
long-running, humorous Mayhem campaign. Lest they be
confused with a brand truly trying to differentiate and be
specific about their position.

When people want to dance, they know what music to
play. When they want to laugh, they know what movies to
watch. When they want a specific experience, or a specific
task to be completed they know what brand to choose, if
they are made aware and provided the understanding.
And when they receive the experience or the outcome
they expected, they tell others.

During a break at an NFL football game this year, the
crowd began going wild during a timeout. It took me a
moment to figure out why. On the jumbotron were the
words making the fans happy.

Dilly Dilly.

Bud Light had been the king of comedy beer commercials
since figuring out the formula in the mid 1980s. Beer makes
people feel good, the ads should also make people feel
good. Through Bud Man, Spuds McKenzie, the frogs,
Whassap?! and dozens of other ideas the brand owned the
position of entertaining beer, the beer of parties and good

times. When they were acquired and restructured as part of the purchase of Anheuser-Busch, Bud Light lost its sense of humor. Sales followed, declining in the face of the tidal wave of craft beer brands popping up in every town in the developed world.

The brand tried to reignite the spark with its core customer base but many had grown up or moved on. Finally they found a new formula. Two throwaway words from a throwback style 30 second spot. Dilly Dilly. The specific customer loves it. For the first time since 2011, Anheuser-Busch Inbev gained share. Both Bud and Bud Light stemmed their declining sales, ticking up in June 2018 once the campaign became fully established. The core audience was coming back.

The campaign has become a rallying cry for celebrating the little things. Cheering life's small victories. And from the sound of 50,000 football fans, they get it. The question is whether the campaign can change the perception of the brand before the catchphrase wears out its welcome. Like 'Wassap,' a popular ad catchphrase have a shelf life. Two years in, and this one is nearing the end of its service. Dilly Dilly is reaching the right people, but isn't telling them anything new about the brand. Brand avoiders aren't put off by it, but will they be sold by it. Can the tagline convince them that the reason they deny the brand is changed or is Bud Light just running sequels? It doesn't tell people how to connect with the brand, how to use it, when to use it. It might just serve as an awareness booster, which unfortunately wasn't Bud Light's problem to begin with.

Nespresso uses their retail locations to serve as a powerful advertisement and reinforcement of its brand. They are found in select geographic areas, to be found in high-end retail environments. Thus aligning the brand immediately with luxury goods and separating from Keurig. The interior design of the stores feel like boutiques, not retailers. Browsing in a Nespresso store makes the brand feel like buying designer clothes as opposed to scanning the racks to grab something at Walmart. By comparison, the competition feels less special. The brand wisely plays into this with price premiums just high enough to separate from competitive coffee makers, adding to the exclusive feel.

Who is the Nespresso designed for? Look at the coffees they feature, it ain't Dunkin' Donuts. Nespresso focuses on espressos and crema, not morning coffee by the pot poured in a travel mug. The brand is clear about the pleasure of coffee and a focus on the exotic elements by using Italian and Latin influenced naming convention. Coffee has been everyday and mundane in the US since the 1800s. This brand is holding it to a higher standard and wants the specific customer to understand. You don't have to have a special occasion to drink Nespresso. Drinking Nespresso *makes it* a special occasion.

This brand was crafted for this customer to help them understand why they would choose the product. It isn't communicating discount prices and traditional product benefits. It is communicating confidence and superiority. Bud Light isn't communicating a product benefit with Dilly Dilly. It is communicating ubiquity. Everyone is invited to laugh at this joke, it is for all of you. Ubiquity is Anheuser-Busch's enemy. It is why bars have stopped carrying it. It is too common. Dilly Dilly reinforces that knowledge, exacerbating the problem.

Readers of this book will be familiar with the four Ps. The idea of the specific brand provides the gravity between product, price, place and promotion that keeps them connected in the consumer's mind. Because Nespresso machines can be found at Target where they are considerably less special than when they are in their own retail surroundings. Yet the price is the same. Nespresso makes the brand desirable so the customer encountering or seeking the product at Target still feels it will provide the luxury they want, even when viewed under fluorescent lights. The motivating insight is not to brew a cup of discount coffee, it is to turn an everyday consumable into a treat.

The cola wars are over. There are too many media channels to have a true head-to-head battle between two brands as Coca-Cola and Pepsi did. But neither of those brands has ever lost focus of its specific customer, despite the knowledge that the best customers for each are occasional consumers of the other.

There is no simple path to gaining mass awareness for the vast majority of brands.

Nespresso is one division of a giant, multinational corporation. It is possible that they could have just positioned Nespresso as what it is, a counter to Green Mountain's Keurig system, designed to sell coffee pods that locks consumers into a subscription model. But that would lead to a war of attrition. Who will cut price? Who will make deals? Nespresso is using the specific model to win with the customers it has recognized would never settle for a Keurig. That is the goal for every company aspiring to become a brand.

What does your specific customer want that only you can provide?

In what way can you serve it that no one else has imagined?

How will you tell the story in a way that feels original?

Simple questions, all. Amazingly, few brands are able to answer honestly when it comes to being truly specific.

SPECIFIC

Specific ©2019 Adam Pierno

This book was reviewed by a collection of volunteers around the world. The following intrepid volunteers went above and beyond to provide special contributions: Sallie Bale, Abbie Love, Lindsey H. Marshall, Quintin Parrish, with special help from Leslie Pierno.

Cover photo: 'Smash' by Jef Poskanzer is used under Creative Commons Attribution Generic 2.0 License: https://en.wikipedia.org/wiki/Creative_ Commons

Guirand Félix. *New Larousse Encyclopedia of Mythology.* Prometheus Press, 1968.
Dru, Jean-Marie. *Disruption.* Village Mondial, 1997.
Barden, Phil. *Decoded: the Science behind Why We Buy.* John Wiley & Sons Ltd., 2013.
Sharp, Byron, and Jenni Romaniuk. *How Brands Grow.* Oxford University Press, 2016.

Hyde, T. S., & Jenkins, J. J. (1969). Differential effects of incidental tasks on the organization of recall of a list of highly associated words. *Journal of Experimental Psychology,* 82(3), 472-481. http://dx.doi.org/10.1037/h0028372
Media average citizen: U.S. census data, Pew Research Center, 2018

Some portions of this book were originally published by *Adweek* and on adampierno.com.

The following articles were used as reference, inspiration or just generally enjoyed during the writing of this book:
https://www.sciencedaily.com/releases/2017/04/170412181341.htm
https://www.collectivebias.com/blog/blog-2016-03-non-celebrity-influencers-drive-store-purchases
https://www.theringer.com/2018/9/4/17816326/all-in-cody-rhodes-young-bucks-nwa-wrestling
https://www.adweek.com/creativity/chilis-our-meals-are-tastier-cardboard-14333/
http://archive.fortune.com/2010/07/02/news/companies/kia_hamsters_advertising.fortune/index.htm
https://digiday.com/retail/davids-bridal-revamping-online-experience-drive-people-stores/